Published by Power of One Publishing

Power of One Publishing
305 1220 Blackfoot Drive
Regina, SK. S4S 6T2
CANADA

I0071653

ISBN 978-0-9880396-1-2
Copyright © 2019 Ken Thiessen

Cover design by Go Giraffe Go Writing & Design Inc, Regina,
SK. CANADA

For information on Power of One Consulting, visit the website, **www.powerofoneconsulting.ca**

DEDICATION

To those who believe it's possible to be entrepreneurial as they lead nonprofit and social sector organizations employing proven business principles to maximize your impact without compromising social responsibility and the organization's core purpose. I hope this book encourages you to keep up the good fight to make a difference in the world! The world needs more people like you committed to transforming communities - one nonprofit at a time!

CONTENTS

ACKNOWLEDGMENTS

How does one adequately begin to recognize the people who have been instrumental in shaping the thoughts which comprise the book you are about to read? It's a perilous and risky journey for sure. The danger is that I will overlook someone who deserves both recognition and gratitude. What follows is my humble and best attempt.

In early 2010 I was given a copy of Verne Harnish's book Mastering the Rockefeller Habits: What You Must Do to Increase the Value of Your Growing Firm. The entrepreneur in me had been contemplating starting my own consulting firm working primarily with nonprofit and social sector organizations. While Verne's book was written for mid-market growth companies, as I read it I knew the principles could easily be adapted to fit the nonprofit and social sector context. When I was given the book, I had no idea how transformative that one seemingly small act of generosity would be! Casey Langbroek, thank you for your generosity of spirit that started with a coffee at Tim Horton's, a copy of a book, an introduction to Keith Cupp and Gravitas Impact Premium Coaches, and an ongoing friendship. Your one act of kindness repeated many times over has made a profound impact in my life that can never be repaid.

Keith Cupp, as the leader of Gravitas Impact Premium Coaches, you have been a mentor, friend, coach, and role model. As our leader you have embodied and modelled the core values of our tribe and have led as a humble servant. I am both inspired and challenged by your life of service to our coaching community. My life is richer because you are a part of it. You believed in me when I didn't believe in myself and you have helped me come to a place where I can once again walk with a sense of confidence in who I am and what I have to offer, not only to my clients but to our Gravitas coaching community. Your authenticity, transparency, and courage to empower others is admirable and legacy building.

Gravitas Certification Training in Orlando, Florida October 2010 resulted in a friendship that I was not expecting. Ted Sarvata you have become a very special part of my life. Who knew where that shared experience would take us, individually and as friends! While we are very different, our friendship has always been based on what we share in common, not on what divides us. That's what true friendship is about. When Marshall Goldsmith challenged us as coaches at a Summit to have a peer coach, we picked each other without ever talking about it in advance! That has led to the formation of our Mastermind group which has grown to include Terry Schaeffer, Sean Evans, Tom Ulbrich and Chris Kenny. Each of you have been instrumental in my own development as a coach and in your own unique way have become good friends. Your input into this book and your encouragement along the way, both in our weekly virtual meetings and our face to face meetings at the Summits have meant so much to me! I know I can count on you to have my back.

Maureen Chan-Hefflin was a source of inspiration and support as we worked on the Four Decisions for the Social Sector v3.2 IP. You primed the pump of imagination and creativity which was rooted in your own understanding of not only the IP but the Social Sector context. Your late night edits and my early morning responses worked synergistically to get the project done in record time without one serious disagreement! Many of the revisions included in the IP are reflected here in this book. You're an inspiration and a friend!

Eric Thielmann you have been a friend who has been there through thick and thin. As we've talked about the idea of this book, it's done more than pass the miles as you've navigated your 18 wheeler across Canada and the U.S. You've understood my heart, the way I think, and the importance of the project. I still owe you for the best piece of advice you've ever given me "They're not your core customer!" DUH!! The coach needed a coach and you were it! Your friendship means so much to me and my life would be left with a gaping hole if you weren't a part of it. Keep fighting the good fight!

Bev, what can I say? Through 35 years of marriage you have supported me along the journey of our life together. There have been unexpected turns along the way, some of them very difficult. I'm the risk taker where you are more cautious. You've joined me in the risks even when you weren't comfortable with them because you wanted to support me in following my dream, my passion and my calling. You challenged me to write and here I am writing a second book. It's all your fault! LOL Thanks for your support, belief in me, and your commitment to me and the work I do.

Chapter 1
Kenaston House - On the Brink

Brad Thomas walked into his office and slouched into his comfortable office chair. Today it didn't feel so comfortable. He was spent! Emotionally, physically, and professionally exhausted. Being the Executive Director of Kenaston House was taking its toll on him and he wasn't sure he had what it took to continue on in his role. Five years of leading a high profile organization in the city but significant challenges behind the scenes was wearing on him. He felt as if he had some big decisions to make. Would he quit, take a medical leave of absence, or suck it up like he had for the last 18 months and keep on going? Those were the options facing him as he sat slouched behind his desk. Picking one was almost more than he could handle.

Kenaston House, a large women's shelter, provided significant services and programs for women with mental health and life skills challenges. Founded 30 years earlier by Nancy Watson, it had grown to the point where it comprised a 40 unit long-term residential apartment building for women with mental health challenges, an adjoining 40 bed short-stay shelter for women dealing with episodic and chronic homelessness, as well as an extensive range of support programs.

Over its 30 year history Kenaston House had grown from the simple, yet bold vision which motivated Nancy to start the organization to the point where it was now a major social service provider in the city. Nancy had retired as the Executive Director a year prior to Brad's hire to lead Kenaston House. While the Board of Directors had been involved in the hiring, their process lacked some of the rigour and structure that would have been common and expected in a corporate setting. The Directors were all well-meaning people, passionate about the worthy work Kenaston House engaged in. What they possessed in passion, they lacked in governance skills. They did their best with what they had but they didn't fully understand the intricacies of running a social sector agency whose annual budget had grown to more than $5 million with a staff of almost 40.

Reviewing applications in the hiring process following Nancy's retirement, Brad's resume immediately peaked the interest of the hiring committee. Brad's history with Kenaston House as a program volunteer certainly didn't hurt. His passion for the work they did reverberated off the pages of his resume. A Program Director with another agency in the city, he was looking for a new challenge. A strong communicator with a compassionate, caring heart for clients in need, he wowed the committee in the interview. The fact he had never managed a staff of 40, or managed an annual budget the size of Kenaston's, or led and implemented a structured planning process didn't seem to be a concern for the committee. He was passionate about the work they did, cared deeply for clients, had a history with Kenaston, and was a strong communicator. That was enough! Apparently it wasn't a concern to the Board either because they offered Brad the job which he immediately accepted.

Brad inherited a team that was a mixed bag in terms of skill set. Jennifer Moore, the strongest member of the team had been hired by Nancy as the CFO just prior to Nancy's retirement. Jennifer was passionate about the work Kenaston engaged in and cared deeply about the clients and the staff team. She possessed strong audit and accounting skills and a breadth of experience in organizations similar to Kenaston House. In many ways, the decision to hire Jennifer would turn out to be Nancy's retirement gift to the organization.

Mary Ridley worked as the Volunteer Coordinator networking with other agencies and groups in the city recruiting volunteers to help staff the many programs operated by Kenaston House. As with most social sector agencies, finding volunteers was an ongoing challenge. What became clear as Brad assumed his role as Executive Director was that one of Mary's key volunteer interview criteria was, "Does this person have a pulse and does it beat passionately for the work we do?" If the answer was "yes" they were recruited. There was one small problem. Pulse and passion didn't always equate with good volunteers, let alone the right volunteers. Ironically, the Board had apparently used the same criteria in hiring Brad. They hadn't asked some of the tougher questions of him either.

Shortly into Brad's tenure as Executive Director, the Program Director resigned. Anxious to flex his Executive Director muscles Brad embraced the challenge of recruiting and hiring a qualified replacement. Karyn Wilson had been a program volunteer with a local community service agency so she knew something about programming. What became clear during the interview was that she shared Brad's passion for programming. Brad seemed unfazed by the fact that she had no previous Program Director experience, offered her the job, and invited her to join the Executive Management Team. Employing an interview and hiring process that was somewhat less than thorough and rigorous was clearly a part of Kenaston's DNA.

Another key development which would prove critical in the governance life of Kenaston House was the resignation of the Chair of the Board of Directors. A close personal friend and ally of Nancy's, he took advantage of Nancy's retirement to transition out himself. He had served in that capacity for a number of years so his exit was not unexpected. As Brad set out to find a new person to serve as Board Chair he immediately thought of Doug Hampton, a long time friend who was the CEO of a large investment firm in the city. Doug had served on other boards and his reputation preceded him. He had a reputation for being a good Board member, worked well with people, and was very good at empowering other people to work within clear parameters and guidelines. He understood the importance of accountability and responsibility and modelled that in his capacity as a leader. Over lunch one day Brad suggested that Doug join the Kenaston Board of Directors as Chair. In typical Doug fashion, he posed some astute and probing questions to Brad relative to the organization's strategic direction, vision, purpose, values, goals and intended outcomes. Brad wooed Doug with his strong communication skills and Doug agreed to join the Board.

Little did Brad realize how the outcome of that lunch would be the best thing for Kenaston House in the long run, or how it would significantly contribute to the escalation of his stress level as Executive Director. Had the dots connected for him back then, it would help explain the complete sense of emotional, vocational, and physical exhaustion he felt. It would provide some context and meaning to the feelings that overwhelmed him as he slouched in his comfortable office chair feeling something far less than comfortable!

Chapter 2
The Nonprofit Challenge - Passion is Not Enough

Kenaston House is not unique when it comes to social sector agencies and nonprofit organizations. While the fuller story of Kenaston House will unfold in the pages ahead, it is a fable. There is no Kenaston House. What isn't fable are the dynamics, experiences, and patterns reflected in the Kenaston House story. Thirty years of experience working in and with nonprofit organizations (and the corresponding scars to prove it) have led me to the point of writing this book. The dynamics, experiences, and patterns you'll encounter as you read on are all grounded in real life. None of these are stand alone experiences. They are patterns I've observed and experienced time and time again, the regularity of which has been saddening, frustrating, and sometimes downright maddening.

While these dynamics, experiences, and patterns evoke a deep emotional response, they are also profoundly motivating! It doesn't have to be this way and it SHOULDN'T be this way! The funding agencies, donors, staff, volunteers, and most importantly the organization's beneficiaries, deserve so much more! So I've committed to use the god-given skills and abilities I have to do something about it! That's not a new commitment - it's one I've been living for a long time but my passion and my energies have become much more focused in the last few years and this book is another manifestation of that passion and commitment.

One of the biggest challenges for social sector agencies and nonprofits is rooted in the founding DNA of the organization. Most of these organizations were started by an individual who was passionate about a cause, an injustice, or a community need. That passion drove them to do something - to make a difference. They shared that passion with others and the ember began to glow brighter, creating other embers, eventually breaking into a full blown fire of enthusiasm and action. Like the saying goes, "The rest is history."

What started off as one person's passion quickly spread to other passionate people and before long a Board was formed. The necessary legal documentation was filed with the appropriate government agency and a new nonprofit organization was birthed. Without that passion, most social sector agencies and nonprofits would remain an idea inside someone's cranium. It's passion that moves the idea from the cranium to the terrarium. But as critical as it is, passion alone isn't enough to start, develop, maintain, and sustain a social sector agency or nonprofit organization let alone grow it! Just like soil by itself isn't enough to grow a healthy plant, passion isn't enough to grow an organization like Kenaston House. It's an indispensable piece of the puzzle but it requires other equally indispensable pieces to turn the puzzle into a masterpiece - a true work of art.

Passion Is Only One of the DNA Molecules

Organizations like Kenaston House have passion as the organizational base DNA molecule, but what brings the organization into existence eventually becomes cancerous unless four other foundational organizational molecules are added to the DNA structure. Those molecules are People, Strategy, Execution and Cash/Funding. These important molecules serve as antigens to the cancerous properties of passion when passion is the lone or primary DNA molecule. When combined with the other foundational DNA molecules, passion becomes a directive force propelling the organization forward in a healthy, aligned, and synergetic fashion resulting in transformed lives, transformed communities, and a better world!

People is about harmony in the organization's culture where staff and volunteers genuinely enjoy working together as a team. In order for that to happen it's essential to implement a robust and disciplined recruiting, hiring, and retention process for staff and volunteers. When those processes are in place and regularly executed with excellence, the calibre and capacity of the team to make a real difference increases exponentially.

Strategy is about gaining clarity and alignment around the long term vision, purpose, and direction of the organization. Strategic thinking helps the executive leadership team focus on things like the 15-20 year vision, core values, core purpose, core competencies, and identifying the organization's core beneficiary. This is absolutely critical because there is a direct correlation between strategic clarity, developing a strong, aligned staff team, and growing a solid donor/funding base.

Execution is about getting things done efficiently and effectively. Execution planning enables the organization to convert strategy into action by articulating organizational, departmental, and individual priorities and metrics each shaped by the strategic thinking component of the process. Being able to deliver prioritized measurable outcomes creates a level of trust and confidence with donors and funding agencies which serves to enhance the organization's ability to deliver on its promise and effect substantive, lasting change.

Cash/Funding is about having sufficient cash flow and cash reserves so that the organization can support existing programs and services and has options to develop and deliver new programs and services. For most social sector agencies this is another critical piece because most struggle for survival, living month-to-month, and in some cases day-to-day.

Can you build a sustainable, growing nonprofit organization on passion alone? You can try, but here's what usually happens to derail the long term viability and impact of the organization.

People

Organizations built on passion as the primary DNA molecule tend to recruit and hire people who possess a deep passion for the cause but don't necessarily have the required skill set for the job they've been hired to do. That applies to the Executive Director, other members of the Executive Management Team, front line workers, and the Board of Directors.

Typically there aren't robust, disciplined recruiting, hiring and retention processes in place. Most often job descriptions are vague, lacking clear accountability structures and performance metrics. This results in the absence of a formal, structured performance review process. How can you evaluate someone without clearly outlined expectations and performance metrics?

Since the people who are typically drawn to work and volunteer for nonprofit organizations tend to be passionate, caring and benevolent people, nonprofit organizations tend to experience greater difficulty in holding people accountable, choosing to err on the side of trust and grace, most often in a manner that exceeds reasonable expectations and standards in the for profit world. The rationale (or excuse) is that these same individuals are not paid as much as they would be in the private sector so the lower standards and expectations are somehow acceptable or even required.

Strategy

Nonprofit organizations tend to take a lot for granted and make a host of assumptions related to strategy. They assume that shared passion automatically translates into clarity around vision, values, and purpose. They assume that shared passion is synonymous with alignment and focus. That is rarely the case!

Nonprofits regularly make the assumption that the strategic planning process is a business principle and since the purpose of the organization is much more "noble" than merely making profit, any processes coming out of the private for-profit world of business must be resisted at all cost! "Remember, we're a nonprofit."

Many nonprofits assume the cause they're fully invested in is far too urgent to "waste" time on a disciplined strategic thinking process. The common refrain is, "We're too busy helping people who really need help to take the time to do that! We can't afford the time! Besides, how would we pay for it?"

While these organizations think they're being effective, they are in essence wandering about somewhat aimlessly making a difference for some, but never really maximizing their impact were they to invest in a disciplined process of strategic thinking.

Execution

Occasionally some nonprofit organizations will engage a strategic thinking process. Most often those processes are facilitated internally by a well meaning Executive Director or Board member. Sometimes they're able to get clarity on the organization's vision, values and purpose but most often that's where the process ends. There is no well articulated execution plan with identified priorities, measurable outcomes, and formal accountability structures. Few within the organization have a clear and tangible sense of how their individual contribution fits with the over-arching organizational vision and priorities. That's one of the primary reasons why these strategic planning exercises fail to deliver much in the way of concrete results and end up collecting dust on a shelf or lost on a server hard drive.

Cash/Funding

A lack of disciplined focus on People, Strategy, and Execution almost always results in a significant funding crisis. That is unless there is a wealthy benefactor bankrolling the organization's operations who never asks the tough, strategic questions.

A lag of rigour and discipline with the other three priorities translates into a lack of rigour and discipline when it comes to monitoring the finances and measuring impact. Most often there is no financial impropriety, just a lack of careful scrutiny and tracking of income and expenses, networking with existing donors and funding agencies, or cultivating new donor and funding sources. Given the aging donor base of most nonprofits, this is a tactical error, the impact of which can only be mitigated by a disciplined process of strategic thinking and execution planning.

Decision Time

Can you start a non-profit organization predominantly on passion? Sure. But growth will be sporadic and reactive at best. Employee turnover will be a significant issue. Measurable outcomes will be circumstantial and anecdotal and alignment will be a dream not a reality. That's the less than good news. But there is good news! It doesn't have to be that way. There are nonprofit leaders who wake up in a cold sweat in the middle of the night terrified that the cause they're fully vested in might unravel and the train might derail. Their sleepless nights and the accompanying angst motivates them to do something. The same passion that drove them to involvement with the organization now motivates them to reach outside themselves, get help, and chart a new and different future. They are few and far between, but they do exist!

So, it's decision time. I'm assuming you are involved in one form or another with a nonprofit or social sector organization. It may be faith based or community based - that matters little. The dynamics, experiences and patterns are the same. If you're a part of a faith based nonprofit let me assure you that the process you're going to encounter in no way violates or contradicts the theological foundation and principles of your organization. In many ways, you've abandoned some of those principles by not being more engaged in a disciplined strategic thinking/execution planning process. You owe it to the people you serve, your donors and funding agencies to operate your organization on more than just passion, a whim, and a prayer.

But it requires you to step out of your comfort zone and risk doing something you've never have done before. It may involve admitting you don't have a clue about how best to engage a strategic thinking/execution planning process or what it might entail. It may involve acknowledging that the very thought of stepping out is terrifying. That you're terrified is not the biggest issue. The biggest issue is whether or not you're going to allow your fear to control you and dictate your behaviour. Or are you going to step into your fear and do what deep down you know you need to do, and do it no matter how terrified you are?

If you're willing to risk stepping out of your comfort zone, ask someone else for help in engaging the unknown of the process, then there's hope for you and your organization. Face your fears, walk into the unknown and keep reading. You're not alone. Others have gone before you and they've lived to experience the thrill of the journey and in the process they've made a huge difference in the lives of the people they were privileged to serve. Like you they cared about their cause but they realized that passion alone wasn't enough. They also came to realize they didn't have to abandon their passion. In many respects, their passion came more alive than they ever dreamed possible. Come along for the ride! It will be worth it. I'm not saying it won't be scary, and I'm not saying it will be easy, but I do guarantee it will be worth it!

Chapter 3
Kenaston House - Trouble Brewing

Sitting at his desk feeling the full weight of his exhaustion, Brad reached for the phone. Even that felt like he was fighting gravity. Doug Hampton's number was in his speed dial and he hit the number. Luckily Doug was in his office and available to take Brad's call. "Doug, I need to see you today. Can we have lunch or coffee? It's important!" Sensing the urgency in Brad's voice but completely oblivious to the issues prompting that urgency, Doug suggested they meet for lunch.

Brad was apprehensive and nervous as he pulled into the restaurant parking lot. That apprehension increased when he spotted Doug's BMW parked close to the door. Brad joined Doug who was already seated in a booth. They reviewed the menu, ordered lunch and then Doug broke the awkward silence. "So what's up? You sounded pretty stressed on the phone!" Brad took a deep breath contemplating what exactly he would tell Doug. "Doug, I'm emotionally, physically, and professionally exhausted and I'm not sure I can keep going!" There he had done it! It was out in the open. He had no clue what would unfold moving forward but his elephant in the room had been identified.

Usually one to mask his internal responses well, the concern on Brad's face was noticeable. "Obviously this hasn't developed overnight. What's brought it to this point and why didn't you let me know you needed help and support?" The 90 minute conversation that ensued covered a host of topics and issues that had been bubbling beneath the surface at Kenaston House for most of Brad's tenure as Executive Director. What Doug learned in that 90 minute conversation was shocking, embarrassing, and telling. Shocking in that he had no clue. Embarrassing because as Chair of the Board of Directors he should have known or at least had processes in place to find out. Telling in the sense that while everything appeared good on the surface, the foundation of Kenaston House was in serious disrepair requiring immediate and drastic attention. But that would have to wait because there were more important issues to attend to - namely the wellbeing of his friend, the Executive Director of the organization Doug was ultimately responsible for.

Doug shifted the attention from the problems brewing at Kenaston to developing a game plan moving forward, one that would first of all provide the support and help Brad needed while ensuring solid leadership on the ground to manage the day to day operations of Kenaston House. Given that there was a good employee benefits plan in place which provided for both short-term and long-term disability, they agreed that Doug would contact the insurance provider to get Brad on short-term disability until such time as medical professionals could determine if long-term disability was required. In addition, Doug agreed to meet with the Executive Management Team and brief them on the developments that had surfaced over lunch. He would also provide the Board an email update and schedule a special Board meeting to develop a more thorough and comprehensive plan moving forward. Neither were prepared for what would unfold in the weeks to come.

As per the decisions made over lunch, Doug emailed the Board members immediately upon his return to the office and scheduled an emergency Board meeting the following week. He also called Jennifer Moore and asked her to schedule an Executive Management Team meeting for the following morning so that Doug could inform them of what he had just learned over lunch.

When Doug arrived at Kenaston House the next morning,

the tension was palpable. Uncertainty filled the air as the Executive Management Team wondered what had occurred to prompt a meeting with the Chair of the Board of Directors. David informed them that Brad would be off for the foreseeable future on a medical leave and that the Board would be meeting the following week to put in place a management plan for the duration of Brad's absence. He advised them that given policies around confidentiality he couldn't go into the specifics other than to say Brad would receive the care and support he needed. David informed them that Jennifer would be in charge until such time as the Board had an opportunity to discuss and finalize a plan moving forward. It wasn't a long meeting, but David's presence certainly raised the stakes in terms of the importance of the meeting. A tsunami of uncertainty had just rolled ashore and over land!

Jennifer remained behind after the rest of the management team had left the meeting and asked David if she could talk to him in private for a few moments. What David was about to hear would only serve to increase the sense of urgency surrounding the Board's involvement in the governance affairs of Kenaston.

Normally a confident, self-assured person, Jennifer was noticeably and uncharacteristically nervous. She began to provide David insight into some of the internal staff dynamics which had been developing for quite a while, dynamics David and the Board were completely unaware of. Jennifer indicated she wasn't surprised Brad was going to be off for a while because he had not been functioning well for quite a while. Brad had been forgetting critical details, avoiding important decisions which needed to be made and had been negligent in supervising and managing the rest of the management team. David was again both shocked and embarrassed. How could these things unfold without he or the rest of the Board having any knowledge of it? He assured Jennifer that the information she had shared with him would be brought to the Board's attention and they would put in place a process not only to address the short term management plan but also a comprehensive organizational assessment to get a more accurate picture of what was really going on at Kenaston House.

David climbed back into his car and drove away deep in thought. In some ways he felt chastised and exposed. Of all people he should have known better to not have the checks and balances in place to help identify some of these important issues before it got to this point. He would never run his own company the way he was running Kenaston House! He knew that the upcoming Board meeting would be pivotal in redefining the management and governance structures and processes moving forward. Given some time to reflect on what he had discovered in his conversation with Jennifer, he asked her to participate in the upcoming Board meeting to brief the entire Board on what she had shared with him. David also knew that the Board would have some questions that he was incapable of answering so Jennifer would be a valuable resource in helping the Board craft a management plan for the immediate future. She would also be able to provide answers to some important financial questions that would invariably be a part of the plan moving forward.

At the Board of Director's meeting the following week, the mood was somewhat pensive and reflective. David informed the Board he had invited Jennifer to attend the meeting given the information she shared with him following his meeting with the Executive Management Team the week previous. David turned to Jennifer and invited her to tell the entire Board what she had shared with him.

As you might expect Jennifer's input evoked a flurry of questions from the Board. What specifically was it about

Brad's behaviour that had caused Jennifer concern? In what ways had Brad abdicated his responsibilities in supervising and managing the Executive Management Team? What important decisions had Brad been avoiding? What they were about to hear would not only shock them but disturb them.

Brad had been mandated by the Board to review all of the staff job descriptions and ensure that all performance reviews had been completed. His report back to the Board had been that these actions "were in process" but Jennifer indicated no action had been undertaken on either the job descriptions or the performance reviews. She also informed them that there had been significant issues with Karyn Wilson's performance as Program Director. While she was a caring, compassionate person, she was ill-suited for the role of Program Director. Brad had been challenged to make a change, but he was paralyzed by fear and procrastination because, "it will hurt her feelings."

What Jennifer would share next would rock the Board to its very core. "I've actually been looking for another job because it's such a horrible environment to work in! I see the incredible potential that we have as an organization but I see how much chaos there is behind the scenes. We're one crisis away from a catastrophe!"

The shocked silence around the Board room table was deafening. Jennifer wasn't sure how to interpret their silence but she cared enough about Kenaston, the staff who worked there, and the women they served to lay it all on the line. What did she have to lose?

Doug was the first to break the silence. "Jennifer, on behalf of the Board, I want to apologize to you. What's become painfully clear over the course of the last week is that we have not done our job as a Board of Directors and in that sense we have failed you and the rest of the staff. It is our job to make sure the right processes are in place AND implemented so that we receive the relevant information we need in order to do our job of governing and do it well. The systems and reporting structures that we have in place are obviously not meeting the minimum threshold related to due diligence and good governance which is clearly our moral and fiduciary duty. One by one other Board members began to speak in support of Jennifer expressing their concern for Brad and Kenaston House as a whole.

With a much clearer understanding of the situation at Kenaston, the Board shifted its attention to developing a plan moving forward. Given what they had just heard from Jennifer, the urgency of a timely and proactive action plan had ramped up significantly.

The first thing they did was address Jennifer's status by reassuring her that now more than ever they needed her skill set and most importantly her perspective, authenticity and her honesty. They had quickly figured out that Jennifer was a valuable member of the Executive Management Team, one they definitely did not want to lose! They probed further as to the internal dynamics which were threatening her long term employment with them. As she continued to fill in more pieces of the puzzle, the picture did not get any prettier. Of the 40 staff, 11 were designated "managers." Most of them did not have the required skill set or experience to be managers but Brad had given them the designation anyway. They were friends of his, they cared about the clients, they were well-intentioned and could be "trained." There was only one problem. Okay, at least one problem. No formal training process existed so staff were left to learn ad hoc on their own. Staff turnover was also at an all time high which was costing Kenaston an incredible amount of money and dramatically impacting employee morale and the quality of program and service delivery.

Needless to say the Board was getting a much clearer picture of how urgent the situation was on the ground at Kenaston House. Jennifer's credibility with them skyrocketed exponentially. They understood the strategic importance of retaining her in the employ of the organization, not only in the interim but long term. She would be a critical resource for them as they sought to develop and implement a proactive management plan moving forward.

As the Board began to discuss next steps, the most immediate need was to designate someone as the interim point leader of the Executive Management Team. In Doug's mind, it was clear that Jennifer should be that person until such time as there was more clarity as to how long Brad would be off on his leave. He asked Jennifer if she would excuse herself from the meeting to give the Board an opportunity to have a brief . conversation. Aware that she might be apprehensive as to what they would talk about, Doug assured her that nothing she had said jeopardized her position with the organization and while he wanted her to excuse herself from the meeting, he did not want her to leave the building. The Board would notify her when they were ready for her to rejoin the meeting.

As soon as Jennifer exited the Board room Doug suggested that the Board seriously entertain the notion of appointing Jennifer as the Interim Executive Director until such time as Brad was ready and able to return. A number of other Board members voiced support for the plan with one Board member making a motion to that effect. It was quickly seconded followed by a brief period of discussion. Doug called for the vote and the vote was unanimous.

Jennifer was invited back into the Board meeting where Doug informed her of the Board's discussion, the motion, and the outcome of the vote. Jennifer was stunned! She thought for sure her honesty would have burned a bridge she could never walk back across again. Instead, it had reinforced the bridge deck and its supports and she had other people walking across that bridge with her - namely the Board. Hesitantly she accepted indicating she would need the ongoing support and help from the Board as she stepped into a role seeking to lead in a way that would be proactive, addressing not only the symptoms of what was going on but more importantly the underlying systemic issues.

The conversation immediately shifted to developing an outline of important next steps in the process of stabilizing the ship they all knew as Kenaston House. Doug suggested that it might be wise for the Board to contract an external consultant who could come in to do an overall assessment of the organization. His rationale was that an external person would see things through a different set of lenses, bring a level of expertise that wasn't present within the organization, and offer a perspective that would be more objective than what any of them as Board members could offer given their involvement in the organizational system.

The immediate response was, "We can't afford it!" which was quickly followed by, "Don't we have someone internal who could do this? What will people think if word gets out that we have problems internally?" Jennifer was chomping at the bit to speak but chose not to, realizing it was a Board matter and they needed to be the ones to debate and own whatever decision they made. Doug was adamant that bringing someone in from the outside was critical to getting the kind of information that would help the Board make the best decision not only for the short term crisis but the long term stability and growth of Kenaston House. Addressing the money question head on, he turned to Jennifer and asked, "Jennifer, what's the state of our finances? Do we have funds that we could allocate to cover the costs associated with contracting an external consultant?" Jennifer indicated that since Brad was going to be on short-term medical leave his salary would be paid by the insurance provider so that money would be freed up within Kenaston's budget and could be allocated for this process. She also indicated that the reputation risk Kenaston faced if the Board didn't respond proactively to deal with the internal crisis was far greater than the expense of bringing in an external consultant and the potential upsides were worth every dollar the Board would invest in the process.

Doug asked if there was a Board member willing to make a motion that the Board contract an external consultant to do an organizational assessment and provide recommendations for a plan of action moving forward. A motion was quickly put on the table and seconded by another Board member. A rigorous discussion ensued with most people speaking in favour of the motion. There were a couple of Board members who struggled. This was not something that nonprofit Boards did! This was something businesses did and Kenaston certainly wasn't a business. One of the questions that emerged related to who the Board could contract to provide the kind of organizational assessment that would really uncover and address the underlying issues. Jennifer offered the name of Tim Kennedy, an independent consultant who worked primarily with nonprofit organizations. She had heard about his work with other social sector agencies in the city and all of the reports gushed with praise for Tim, his approach, methodology, recommendations and outcomes. Doug had heard of Tim as well, but had no first hand experience or exposure to Tim or organizations who had accessed his consulting services. Allowing adequate time for discussion, Doug called for the vote and the vote was 6-2 in favour of the motion. The Board asked Doug to contact Tim, outline the situation, and request a proposal for consulting services so that the Board could allocate the required funds and initiate the process.

Doug left the meeting with a deep and profound awareness of the magnitude of the task that lay ahead of them as a Board. Little did he know the challenges they would have to address as a Board or the magnitude of those challenges. Jennifer, on the other hand, left the Board meeting with a renewed sense of hope. What she had suffered through in silence was now out in the open and she actually had hope the Board was going to do something about it. Perhaps she would stop trolling the job websites and fully invest herself in helping Kenaston House realize its incredible potential. She was not going anywhere, at least not yet. She would let the process unfold and see how the Board responded moving forward before she made any decision regarding her long term employment at Kenaston House.

Chapter 4
Reality - Sad But True

It wouldn't be a surprise if disbelief describes your reaction to the latest chapter in the saga at Kenaston House. I get that! It sounds stranger than fiction, but it's NOT! You can't make this stuff up! I've seen this scenario played out time and time again as I've worked with nonprofit organizations and social sector agencies. Well-meaning Board members naively believing that everything is order, completely unaware they're sitting on an organizational fault line with an earthquake of epic proportions about to significantly shift the landscape.

There are several factors which contribute to this reality. The "we're a nonprofit" notion is a pervasive, counterproductive, and harmful perspective that influences most non-profit organizations. The statement masks some deeply held, albeit unhealthy core values within the world of nonprofits. Sometimes these core values audibly shatter the silence but most often they're never verbalized. The fact that they're not verbalized in some ways intensifies the powerful grip they have on the organization. If you don't know what's driving your actions and attitudes, how can you ever change them? So what are some of the core values masked in that statement?

Core Value #1

"How you run a nonprofit is completely different than how you run a business."

REALLY? SERIOUSLY? Your nonprofit has annual revenue of $5 million and somehow you think that you're justified to look at that revenue, spend that revenue, track that revenue, identify and measure your outcomes differently than the for profit business down the street from you that generates the same annual revenue? As a nonprofit, you are an employer bound by the same labour laws as that for profit business. You probably use the same financial institution as many businesses do. You do your bank deposits the same way they do. You use accounting software just like a business does to track revenue and expenditures. If you don't you should! You have many of the same bills to pay every month as your for profit business neighbour. You have physical infrastructure like a building, office equipment and furniture, to maintain. You have utility bills to pay.

The notion that somehow a nonprofit is run fundamentally different than a for profit business is not only a flawed myth but a dereliction of duty on the part of those responsible for the management and governance of the organization. Granted the cause *may* be more "noble" in that the programs and services of most social sector agencies address significant human needs, problems and issues. I would contend then that those tasked with the management and governance of the organization owe it to their funding partners, donors, staff, volunteers, and most importantly their beneficiaries to run the organization based on the most solid business principles and best practises available to them so as to maximize their positive impact in doing good in the world! Surely the cause is worthy of that discipline, rigour, and commitment!

What I find somewhat surprising as I work with nonprofit boards and Executive Management Teams is that often influential and successful business people like Doug sit as Board members of the organization. The reason for their success is that they employ solid business fundamentals and best practises in their vocational for profit endeavours. They hold people accountable to achieve predetermined measurable outcomes. But a metamorphosis occurs in the space of time between leaving their place of business and entering the Board meeting of the nonprofit. Their business expertise and skill seem to evaporate into thin air. In the exercise of their fiduciary duty as trustees of the organization they tolerate and advocate for practises that would never be tolerated in their businesses. A friend on mine who left the world of nonprofits to become a successful entrepreneur once said to me, "As a business owner, I fire people for less that what I was expected to tolerate, condone, AND accept as a nonprofit Executive Director." Unfortunately, that is a sad and all too true reflection of reality in many nonprofits.

Core Value #2

"We don't pay them as much as they could make in the private sector so we can't really expect as much from them."

The most dangerous aspect of this core value is that there is a kernel of truth in the statement. Nonprofits rarely pay people what they could earn in the for profit world. There is no disputing that as a fact. But, the notion that somehow that fact ought to translate into lowering the expectations, job requirements and skill sets for individuals in the employ of a nonprofit organization is fallacious and ultimately foolish. Don't the people served by the organization deserve the assurance that there are solid standards and expectations in place AND enforced on those employed by the organization? Do the donors and funding partners not deserve the assurance that their hard earned dollars are going to be utilized by the most competent and caring people who are held accountable to deliver measurable outcomes within the parameters of the vision, values, and purpose of the organization?

The other place where this value rears its ugly head in the context of nonprofit organizations is the attitude towards volunteers. It closely parallels the attitude many nonprofits have toward staff. Typically less than acceptable performance from volunteers is tolerated for similar reasons. "They're just volunteers" is a common, equally unhelpful refrain. This core values leads nonprofits to settle for second or third best (and sometimes even worse). As a result the organization and everyone associated with it suffers. And it drives the good staff and volunteers away! People like Jennifer.

Core Value #3

"We're about changing lives not counting numbers."

Inherent in this core value is an anti metrics sentiment as if somehow life transformation or community impact and metrics are mutually exclusive. There's no doubt that developing qualitative metrics to measure life transformation or community impact is a more complex and complicated process than developing metrics to measure tangibles like dollars in, dollars out, meals served, or the number of people who access your agency's services. But without some quantifiable metrics, how do you define and measure what success looks like for your organization? Unfortunately this core value is an excuse to avoid the more difficult task of developing the qualitative metrics that not only help outline what success looks like but also keep the organization and those within it accountable to outcomes not just activity.

How this works its way through the organization is that since there are no overarching metrics to measure how the organization is doing, there are oftentimes no metrics to measure how individuals within the organization are doing. In some sense it's about whether or not an individual shows up and stays busy while they're on duty. Unfortunately, busyness does not necessarily equate with "success" or impact!

Core Value # 4

"We're a nonprofit - we can't afford it!"

Most nonprofits start from a basis of scarcity not abundance. They would never categorize it as such but when you strip away the veneer of their feigned fiscal responsibility, you quickly realize that the core value has less to do with responsible stewardship of the financial resources and more about a flawed mindset.

Dan Pallota in his thought provoking book "Uncharitable" aggressively challenges this notion in a way that I tend to agree with. The assumption that staff should accept less by way of pay, that little money should be spent on marketing and administration, that recycled or past generation computers and IT technology are good enough, or that no external professionals should be contracted in many ways flies in the face of business best practises. Sometimes the very people who advocate for these notions are Board members who would find it unconscionable to run their businesses by the same core values.

Some of the questions that are rarely asked are, "Can we afford not to do it?" "What's it costing us to maintain the status quo?" and, perhaps most importantly, "Would the expenditure of this money better help us serve our clients, live out our values, vision, and purpose?"

Each of these core values are alive and well in the organizational culture of Kenaston House. There's never been a meeting of any Executive Management Team or Board of Directors where they formally adopted these core values and yet they exert incredible power and influence within the organization. If you were to name these as their operating core values there would be strong and defiant resistance from everyone within the organization. This represents a significant organizational blind spot in desperate need of enlightenment and exposure.

What if instead of starting from a baseline of scarcity a nonprofit started from a baseline of abundance? What if they asked the questions above and did the hard work of answering them honestly? How would things be different? How might that change the conversations? The plans? The organizational decisions? Budgeting process? Hiring process?

As you reflect on your nonprofit or social sector agency, which of these core values are alive and well in your organization? How are they negatively impacting your organizational culture and limiting your effectiveness in serving the people who access your programs and services? If you were to expose these core values to others in your organization what would the reaction be? Would anybody take you seriously or would they marginalize or label you as a troublemaker?

Chapter 5
Kenaston House - Help is On the Way

Two days after after the Board meeting Doug and Tim Kennedy met over lunch to discuss the current situation at Kenaston House and develop some idea as to what a consulting process might look like and what the outcomes of such a process would be. The more they talked the more Doug was drawn to Tim. He could tell that Tim had a good business sense along with a deep understanding of the world of non-profits. That caught Doug off guard because he wasn't expecting it, but it was hard to ignore or disregard what Tim was saying because it made so much sense. Doug was embarrassed (again) that he hadn't thought of this on his own. He certainly knew a lot of what Tim was saying from the standpoint of running his investment business but he had never thought of implementing those same principles and practices into the governance structure at Kenaston House.

As Doug talked Tim did a lot of listening and asked a few strategic questions, questions for which Doug couldn't provide good, solid answers. The nature of Tim's questions only served to increase Doug's respect for him because he was asking the kinds of questions that exposed some significant systemic flaws and gaps in Kenaston's processes.

After an hour of dialogue and interaction, Doug suggested that Tim put together a formal proposal outlining several components of what a consulting engagement might look like along with a timeline and fee structure. Tim suggested several general components which he thought might identify some of the underlying dynamics impacting Kenaston House. The first was an organizational culture inventory. This would involve the participation of the entire staff and management team using an online survey platform. Their input would provide a good overview of how those most deeply connected to Kenaston House felt about the organization. The information from this survey could prove to be a valuable resource for the Board moving forward. In addition, Tim suggested that he conduct a structured one-on-one interview with each of the Executive Management Team. Given the nature of the conversation over lunch and Doug's inability to provide solid answer to some of the questions related to vision, values, and purpose, Tim suggested that a formal planning process would also be helpful to outline the long term direction, identify organizational priorities, and create a sense of alignment between the Executive Management Team and the Board, and within the organization as a whole. Doug agreed that a proposal outlining these components in more detail would be helpful as the Board contemplated a plan of action moving forward.

Within 24 hours of their lunch meeting, Doug had a formal proposal from Tim in his inbox. Impressed by the promptness of Tim's proposal, he circulated it immediately to all of the Board members. While Doug wasn't surprised by the $48,000 price tag associated with what Tim was proposing, he knew that some of the Board members would be taken aback by it. Given the urgency of initiating a process he arranged a conference call for that evening so the Board could discuss the proposal and make a decision. The meeting went relatively well however, there were some on the Board who resorted to the "we can't afford this" mantra. Doug's question in response was, "What will it cost us not to engage this process?" Finally one of the Board members made a motion that the Board engage Tim's services as outlined in the proposal and that Tim commence his work as soon as possible. The motion was seconded, and passed with a 6-2 vote.

Within 10 days Tim had the online organizational culture

inventory ready to go and the consulting process began in earnest. All staff and Executive Management Team members were invited to participate in the survey and the response rate was a resounding 95%. That provided a high degree of validity to the results. As well, Tim conducted one-on-one in person interviews with each member of the Executive Management Team.

The picture that emerged was more drastic than Tim had realized. He knew there were problems but some troubling themes and patterns emerged from the organizational culture inventory and the personal interviews. Tim knew that no matter how strong Kenaston's reputation was in the city, the foundation that reputation rested on was in complete disrepair. His challenge would be to compile the results in a report that wouldn't devastate the Board but would still paint an honest and accurate picture for them. The other challenge would be to offer recommendations that would move beyond window dressing and tinkering to address the deeper systemic issues. He was up to the challenge because those were two of his strengths. He knew that Doug and the Board would be surprised by what they were about to discover.

Tim's report summarized the key issues identified in the organizational culture inventory and the interviews.

• Most of the staff indicated they would not recommend Kenaston as a good place to work.

• There was little correlation between job promotions and individual competence or skill.

• Hiring processes were not deemed to be fair and impartial.

• The Program Staff indicated overwhelmingly there were issues with Karyn, their direct supervisor. That corresponded with feedback that surfaced in the individual interviews with Karyn's colleagues on the Executive Management

Team.

• Paid staff who had interaction with volunteers overwhelmingly identified significant concerns with Mary, the Volunteer Coordinator. Again those comments corroborated with information gleaned in the interviews with her colleagues on the Executive Management Team.

• None of the staff had current job descriptions and most had not had a formal performance review in over 3 years.

• Perhaps most surprising was the complete lack of confidence expressed by staff and the Executive Management Team in Brad and his leadership abilities.

• There was no clear sense of what the long term strategic plan was for Kenaston nor how individual activities tied in with Kenaston's long term plan.

• While Kenaston had identified core values, the staff indicated the core values were not lived out by the majority of the Executive Management Team nor were they enforced throughout the organization.

• Brad had a pattern of avoiding conflict which only exacerbated the conflict.

• While Jennifer had sought to implement solid accounting and financial processes and systems, she had been thwarted at almost every turn by Brad.

• The only positive that emerged out of the culture inventory and the individual interviews was Jennifer's contribution to the team. The comment that kept surfacing was, "If it wasn't for Jennifer, we'd be in a lot more trouble than we're in."

As Tim reviewed the results and began compiling his report, he knew the shock value was going to be significant when the Board read through it but he held nothing back in his report. He was honest, succinct but sensitive in how he framed not only his findings, but also his recommendations.

He outlined five key recommendations:

- A one day in service with the Executive Management Team to review the results of the organizational culture inventory.
- Subsequent to that, Brad, Karyn, and Mary should be transitioned out with accompanying reasonable severance packages.
- Retaining Jennifer should be the highest Board priority and her management responsibilities and authority within in the organization increased.
- A recruiting process should commence immediately for a new Executive Director. The new Executive Director MUST have a proven track record of successfully leading a social sector agency similar to Kenaston as Executive Director. This should be a non-negotiable.
- A formal strategic planning process be engaged immediately upon hiring a new Executive Director to begin the process of charting the long term direction of Kenaston House. This process would be ongoing over the course of the following year at which time it should be re-evaluated by the Board to determine whether it continuing beyond the 12 month time period would be both advisable and beneficial to solidify and continue to build on the work accomplished in year one.

Just as Tim was working on the final draft of his report, he received a call from Doug inquiring as to the status of the report and wondering if they could schedule a breakfast meeting to discuss it. Tim indicated he was putting the finishing touches on the report and it would be emailed to him within the hour. They agreed to meet for breakfast the following morning.

Tim wasn't sure what to expect when he arrived the next morning. They ordered breakfast and then Doug looked at

Tim and said, "That's the most direct and forthright report I've ever read." That did little to calm Tim's anxiety and he wasn't quite sure if Doug's comments were a good thing or a bad thing. Doug continued, "We knew we had some challenges, but we didn't know we had a crisis. We clearly have a crisis." From there the conversation quickly turned to the heightened sense of urgency which demanded swift and decisive action from the Board. Doug agreed that time was of the essence and asked if Tim could be available to meet with the Board to debrief them regarding the findings and recommendations contained in the report. Tim agreed it would be advisable for him to meet with the Board to assist them in their decision making process and answer any questions related to the report. Tim offered Doug several times that worked on his calendar and encouraged Doug to confirm a meeting time and date once he had consulted the Board. Doug assured Tim that he would be strongly advocating the Board's adoption of the report along with ALL of the recommendations.

While Doug recognized the magnitude of the challenges that lay ahead for Kenaston House and the Board, he was in an odd way energized by the thought of taking on the challenge! He was impressed with Tim's honesty and candour and looked forward to working with him moving forward. He wondered if Tim could also help him in his investment firm but that was a conversation for another day.

Chapter 6
Culture Change Starts at the Top or it Doesn't Start!

Every organization has its own unique culture, an inherent system of norms and values that shape and define how the organization operates. Whether it's a nonprofit organization or a for profit business, every organization reflects the cultural norms and values that the leader either passively enables or actively promotes. If there's a culture problem in your organization, all roads lead back to the leader. For better or for worse. And that's not just the Executive Director! It goes right back to the Board of Directors as well.

Some Board members might balk at that notion, but think about it this way. If the Executive Director is either passively enabling or actively promoting organizational cultural norms and practises that are counterproductive and incongruent with what you would expect the norms and practices to be in a thriving and healthy organization, then the Board has to own that because they have the ultimate responsibility to supervise, monitor, and manage the Executive Director. Board ignorance as to what's really going on in the day to day operations of the organization is no excuse! Board's have a moral and legal duty to KNOW what's going on and if they don't know it's their job to put in place mechanisms to find out. Once they're aware of what's going on, if they do nothing about it, they are complicit in the perpetuation of an unhealthy organizational culture.

Most often the current cultural values and norms didn't emerge out of a profound offsite planning session that generated unanimous buy-in, passion and commitment. They evolved over time with little, if any, reflective evaluation. Which begs the question, "When was the last time you as an executive leadership team (staff AND Board) invested the time and energy to do some reflective evaluation on your organizational culture?"

The longer the time frame between intentional, reflective evaluation of your organizational culture, the greater the commitment to maintain the status quo by those within the system. A "good" crisis, a key leadership exit or transition, or the arrival of a new team member can often destabilize the comfortable sense of equilibrium and provide the organization an opportunity for reflective evaluation and focused action to bring about culture change. Destabilization is not always a bad thing. Sometimes it's advantageous for a leader to initiate the destabilization process for the long term good of the organization. But that takes courage, because quite likely you'll have to change how you lead! There are a host of good culture assessment tools available to assist you in the process but here's a simple process you can initiate internally to prime the culture pump.

So what are some of the factors that contribute to an unhealthy organizational culture? Perhaps the biggest factor is an Executive Director or key point leader who consistently fails to "walk the talk" and who isn't held accountable for his or her "walk." Whether it's failing to model and enforce the organizations core values, or identify and hold individuals accountable to clear, measurable and specific outcomes, or tolerating underachievement and substandard performance and outputs either personally or from others within the organization, that's a sure-fire guarantee that before long those behavioural patterns and performance standards will become the norm rather than the exception within the organization. That's why a regular, intentional, and reflective organizational culture self assessment and evaluation process is critical to prevent atrophy from setting in.

However, this comes with a strong caveat. Culture change

is hard work. No bones about it! Once unhealthy organizational patterns have taken root, the roots are difficult to extract. Those patterns become the organizational thistles and quack grass, and the longer the patterns have been passively tolerated or actively promoted, the more difficult it is to extract the culture weeds. Extracting them requires an industrial strength organizational weedkiller and even then the culture weeds do not die willingly or easily! Organizational systems have a pervasive and inherent commitment to maintain the status quo. Change the players on the team, and things pretty much stay the same. Unhealthy patterns persist, the organization's impact is muted and stunted and life continue on as "normal." That's because organizational culture issues are always bigger than any one person or department. There may be one person who embodies some of the unhealthy cultural norms and practises but it's never an individual issue. It's always an organizational issue and that's another reason why culture change is so hard to bring about.

You're probably beginning to get a clearer picture why organizational culture change has to start at the top if it's going to happen at all. Unfortunately, often the person at the "top" is the biggest impediment to real culture change. Sometimes he's unaware of the unhealthy cultural realities that stifle the organizational functioning. Sometimes he's just resistant to change himself. If he reports to a Board, the Board has passively enabled those patterns to persist unchecked and the Board are the ones who must take decisive action to assess the current culture, mandate culture change, model it themselves, and put in place accountability structures to measure progress in the culture change process. That requires courage, persistence, and determination.

So what are some of the steps you as a leader can do to find out the status and state of your organization's culture? What are some of things that Doug and the Board at Kenaston House could have done that might have provided valuable insights which could have helped them be more proactive in addressing the underlying issues?

An employee engagement survey is usually a relatively simple process to implement but one that can yield a wealth of valuable information. There are a host of good online resources available that could be structured using one of a number free online survey tools. These surveys should be anonymous to ensure honest feedback from staff. Depending the size of your organization, you might want to identify departments within the organization so that you can more accurately determine the "trouble" spots. Had Kenaston employed this kind of survey they quite likely would have become aware of some of the challenges related to Brad, Karyn, the Program Director, and Mary, the Volunteer Coordinator.

It doesn't have to be a complicated process or survey. Asking two simple questions in an online survey format can yield valuable information.

"What One or Two Things About Our Culture Keep You With the Organization?" Asking your employees to identify the one or two thing about your culture that keep them with your organization and make them want to stay can be a very informative exercise! As a leader, there is a zero cost investment but this exercise has the potential to produce an incredible high Return on Investment that will impact your bottom line! Quite likely, it already makes a positive difference in your bottom line.

"What One or Two Things About Our Culture Make It Harder For You To Stay?" But asking your employees to also identify the one or two things about your culture that make it harder for them to stay, that might even make them surf the job posting websites is another critical exercise. Again, it's a zero cost investment, other than perhaps your pride depending on the responses to the question but if you're a leader who's serious about engaging your team and fostering a learning culture within your organization, what you'll probably discover is that this reality is also affecting your bottom line - negatively! Whether you realize it or not, the things about your organizational culture that make your employees even CONSIDER leaving means you're probably not getting their best work. At the very least they're holding something back and/or casting a wandering glance at another job opportunity. That too has an impact on your bottom line and it's not positive.

Here's the rub. If you as a leader aren't prepared to first of all take a hard look in the mirror and ask yourself the question, "To what degree, and how do I contribute to the healthy AND unhealthy cultural dynamics of our organization?" and then do something to change your behaviour, there's little hope for cultural change in your organization. If you don't already have a good coach, get one, particularly one who can be a confidante - someone who will tell you what you NEED to hear, not just what you WANT to hear. It really is all up to you as the leader to model the new cultural reality that you want and reasonably expect your people to live into. Culture change starts with the leader or it doesn't start at all! Initiate the change for the good of your organization - for the good of your people - for the good of your beneficiaries, donors and funding agencies, your staff, and your community! Don't they deserve at least that much from you as a leader?

The Board of Directors at a client I worked with implemented an employee engagement survey as a part of the Executive Director's performance review process. Since the Executive Director was the only staff person who attended Board meetings, the Board wanted to have a more comprehensive sense of how things were going within the staff team. The results were astounding. The Board discovered that most of the staff did not rate their organization as a good place to work. The Executive Director received very poor ratings from his staff in terms of his communication with them. A number of the staff openly acknowledged they weren't giving their best effort at work. The vast majority of the staff expressed that they had no idea how their individual activities tied in with the overall vision of the organization. When the Board received the results they were stunned. Needless to say the next Board meeting had added intensity and focus as they reviewed the results with the Executive Director. He was asked to provide a clear action plan to the Board within 5 days outlining how he was going to address the concerns raised in the employee engagement survey. In addition the Board informed him that they would conduct a formal performance review within 90 days. The Executive Director failed to meet the 5 day deadline and when he eventually submitted his action plan to the Board, it was so vague and nonspecific that it was rejected outright by the Board. The strong action of the Board was the first step in significant culture change in that organization and at the 90 day performance review the Executive Director was informed that his employment was being terminated.

So what about your organization? Do you have the courage as an organization to take a look in the mirror and let the mirror reflect your reality back to you? If not, what's it costing you to avoid facing your reality? There is a cost whether you realize it or not. There's a human cost, financial cost, and most importantly an impact cost.

Chapter 7
Kenaston House - A Painful Look in the Mirror

As soon as Doug got back to his office, he circulated Tim's report to the full Board with with a "Viewer Discretion Advised" caveat and a suggested date for a Board meeting to discuss the report and the recommendations contained in it. He also indicated he had invited Tim to be present to walk through the report and answer questions the Board might have. He knew they would be just as shocked as he was but this was a time to take a painful, honest look in the organizational mirror.

Before the day was out, Doug had received phone calls from several members of the Board. They were indeed just as shocked as he had anticipated. Some were shocked at how direct and forthright Tim had been in the report, and every caller expressed shock at how unaware they had been of what was really going on at Kenaston House. None of the callers rejected the report's finding and recommendations out of hand. Two Board members were shocked at the cost of the consulting process but given their responses to earlier decisions that was one thing that didn't shock Doug!

Every Board member was present when Doug called the meeting to order. Doug introduced Tim to the rest of the Board and then turned the meeting over to Tim who walked through the report in more detail expanding on some of the more critical aspects of the report's findings. He chose to review the recommendations before opening it up for questions because he knew that the two were so inextricably linked that it was best to give them the full picture before taking their questions.

The questions came quick and fast. Each questioner prefaced their question with an expression of appreciation for

Tim's work and the information included in the report. While some of the questions related to issues uncovered related to the day to day management of Kenaston, as many questions focused on the Board's role in enabling the situation to deteriorate to the point it was now at.

As Tim responded to the questions he was as forthright and direct in person as he had been in the report. He wasn't rude or hurtful - just incredibly honest in his efforts to help the Board face the brutal facts as they had emerged in the assessment process. He was cautiously hopeful that they would have the courage to make the difficult decisions that would help set Kenaston on a much healthier path moving forward.

As expected, one Board member raised the matter of Tim's fees for the process moving forward as he had outlined in his report. The individual was shocked at the proposed costs associated with the process and wondered aloud how Kenaston could afford to engage such a process. Tim was prepared for the question and asked a question in response. "What do you think these issues are costing you now as an organization?" That was quickly followed by a second question, "If word got out about what's really going on behind the scenes at Kenaston, what do you think the potential impact would be in terms of your donors and funding partners?" Most of the Board avoided eye contact because they all knew the answer to his questions. It was costing them a whole lot more than they realized in terms of lost productivity, staff turnover, and lack of alignment and focus. They didn't even want to think about what impact a news leak might have on their donor and funding revenue stream. They knew the results would be significant and it would take them a long time to rebuild the lost credibility. What had taken so long to establish would evaporate in a heartbeat if they didn't do something decisive and proactive in response to the findings of the report they held in their hands.

After significant discussion had taken place, Doug asked if someone on the Board was willing to make a motion relative to the report. Heather Simpson, the CEO of a lighting company in the city made a motion that the Board receive the report and adopt all of the recommendations included in it. That was seconded by Mark Stevens, the Vice President of a large Credit Union. There was a brief discussion and then Doug called for the vote. Unlike the two previous votes, the Board was unanimous in approving the motion.

With the report and recommendations fully embraced by the Board, the conversation quickly turned to developing an implementation plan.

One by one Tim reviewed each of the recommendations outlining the rationale and offering some input as to the order of priority and a process as to how the Board might want to implement each of the recommendations. Given the fact that three of the recommendations related to terminating staff, significant discussion ensued related to the logistics surrounding notice, severance, and benefits. The sentiment that prevailed in the conversation was the desire to be both fair and generous with Brad, Karyn and Mary in recognition that the Board shared some responsibility for not having the appropriate processes in place that would have surfaced these realities sooner. Given the intricacies of the situation, the Board agreed they should access a legal opinion to ensure that the Board didn't expose themselves to undue liability and risk because of a lack of due diligence on their part.

Having put in place a reasoned process for dealing with the recommendations related to personnel, the discussion shifted to the recommendation related to a planning process. As Tim outlined for the Board what the process might entail, the items to be addressed in each segment of the process, and how it might unfold over the course of the next year, more than one Board member had an noticeable puzzled look on their face. Tim probed further as to their sense of puzzlement. One by one of the Board members indicated that while they used these kinds of processes in their vocational life, it had never crossed their minds that a similar process might be an integral component of good governance at Kenaston House. Tim was taken aback by the fact that some of these Board members who were very competent business people had not connected the dots between what they did in their vocational life with their governance role at Kenaston House.

Not only would it be beneficial for Kenaston House in terms of the day to day management of the organization, it would give much needed substance to the credibility they already possessed. It would also instil confidence in their donors and funding partners, and most importantly it would benefit the people served through their programs and services. The more Tim outlined the benefits of engaging such a process and connecting the dots for the Board, the more the excitement level ramped up in the room. As significant as the challenges were, there was a sense that in the midst of the emerging chaos, they were on the brink of something significant that would dramatically impact the future of Kenaston in a positive way and propel it to new levels of impact in the city.

Following extensive discussion, the Board agreed to an action plan moving forward. They agreed that Doug and one other Board member would meet with Kenaston's lawyer to get a legal opinion on how best to proceed with the staffing transitions in a manner that wouldn't expose Kenaston to any risk or legal liability. The Board was adamant that whatever staffing transitions were a part of the plan moving forward, the people being transitioned out deserved to be treated fairly and in accordance with the relevant employment laws in effect in their jurisdiction. In terms of a stop gap measure to address the short team implications on the day to day operations, it was agreed that Doug, Heather Simpson and Mark Stevens meet with Jennifer to inform her of the Board's decisions and solicit her input on putting in place an interim management team and plan to ensure as little interruption to the day to day operations at Kenaston House.

The Board also requested that Doug, Heather and Mark serve as an ad hoc Human Resources Committee and that they engage the services of an Employment Agency to begin the search for a new Executive Director. Given their governance structure, the Board delegated all other staff hires to the Executive Director. The Board was adamant that they wanted the process to be rigorous and thorough. They were unwavering in their position. They were more interested in getting the right person for the position even if it meant an elongated process. If they had learned anything they had learned that they needed to be much more engaged and aware of what was going on in the day to day management and they needed to make sure that they had the right person in the position of Executive Director. Once they had that person in place they would empower that individual to recruit and hire a new Volunteer Coordinator and Program Manager.

The Board also agreed that once the new Executive Director had been hired, they would finalize the dates with Tim to begin the strategic planning process. Since the new Executive Director would be a key contributor to the plan and be tasked to implement it, they agreed that they would wait until that person was in place before they finalized the dates. This was more a matter of good governance than a delaying tactic. They were unanimous in their agreement that it was imperative they engage a formal planning process. To ignore or reject that recommendation contained in Tim's report would be irresponsible on their part as a Board.

While the report had been shocking and the meeting difficult, as a Board they had taken a painful look in the mirror,
they had faced the brutal facts, and they had turned an important corner that would take them in a new direction not only
as a Board but as an organization. The challenges that lay
ahead were significant but the Board was united and functioning in a way that was unprecedented in recent history. In a
rather odd way, there was a new sense of excitement about
their work together and the future of the organization.

Chapter 8
Reality Check - Courage to Face the Brutal Facts

Jim Collins, in his book Good to Great, brought the Stockdale Paradox to the forefront for many business leaders. James Stockdale, one of the highest ranking U.S. military officers ever to be held prisoner of war in Vietnam was interviewed by Collins about his experience as a prisoner of war. Stockdale was subjected to incredible atrocities yet he emerged from his experiences stronger than when he was taken captive. When asked by Collins what his coping strategy was Stockdale said, "I never lost faith in the end of the story, I never doubted not only that I would get out, but also that I would prevail in the end and turn the experience into the defining event of my life, which, in retrospect, I would not trade." Collins pressed him further inquiring as to those who didn't make it out. Stockdale's response was somewhat surprising, not what you would expect. "Oh, that's easy, the optimists. Oh, they were the ones who said, 'We're going to be out by Christmas.' And Christmas would come, and Christmas would go. Then they'd say, 'We're going to be out by Easter.' And Easter would come, and Easter would go. And then Thanksgiving, and then it would be Christmas again. And they died of a broken heart." Stockdale then went on to share what might have been the most significant lesson learned during his time in a Prisoner of War Camp, "This is a very important lesson. You must never confuse faith that you will prevail in the end—which you can never afford to lose—with the discipline to confront the most brutal facts of your current reality, whatever they might be."

Most people can't comprehend what it must have been like for Stockdale to live seven and a half years in captivity. Even fewer can imagine surviving that length of time in captivity. But Stockdale's secret was his ability to face the brutal facts about his situation. He didn't pretend they were any better or any worse than what they were in reality. That took incredible courage on his part. But more than courage, it took an undying faith that no matter how difficult his current reality was, he would prevail in the end.

Many nonprofit leaders and boards do not possess the courage to face the brutal facts - either about their own leadership style and impact or the true state of affairs in the organizations they're tasked to lead. Even when faced with the brutal facts, seemingly capable and competent leaders repeatedly AND willfully choose to deny, ignore, or refute their reality and the brutal facts. Margaret Heffernan calls it "willful blindness."

In my experience, few leaders or Boards demonstrate the courage manifested by the Kenaston Board. They were willing to face the brutal facts and then respond in a proactive way to address their reality rather than ignore, deny, or refute the facts. It would have been easy to direct a barrage of arrows at Tim, the messenger. It's always easier to shoot the messenger than it is to look in the organizational mirror and acknowledge the brutal realities calling for leadership attention. Like James Stockdale, this requires a depth of character and courage that has been finely tuned and honed over the years leading up to the crisis. Crisis has a way of exposing character not developing character. That's not to say that crisis doesn't refine and hone our character, but first and foremost, crisis reveals character - for better or worse.

The very fact they contracted Tim's consulting services demonstrates a level of courage and self-awareness on the part of the Board that is rare in nonprofit circles. Good leaders, and good Boards are not afraid to secure outside help and perspective. Vanity and pride does not keep them trapped in the bubble of naive, self-protection. Not only did they have the courage to contract Tim's services, they saw it as an investment in the long term health and future of the organization. Even if it wasn't in the their annual budget they were committed to find a way to cover the associated costs because they knew that the costs of inactivity - doing nothing - were potentially far greater that Tim's consulting fees. That was without the human costs associated with having people who lacked the required skill set and as such were not well-positioned in the organization.

Hearkening back to my experience working with nonprofit organizations, many nonprofits are afraid to ask for help. They'd rather muddle along doing the best they can with the resources they have, accepting status quo as "good enough" and hiding behind the notion that "we're a nonprofit" as if that somehow absolves them of the responsibility and need to do the hard work of facing the brutal facts and executing with excellence. Most are equally unwilling to view accessing external resources as an investment in the long-term health and sustainability of the organization. While most nonprofit leaders and Board member would never express it this way, they are in effect prepared to sacrifice the quality of program and service delivery to their beneficiaries rather than face their own fears by taking a look in the organizational mirror, facing the brutal facts for what they are, and then committing to a proactive action plan to address them. Apart from a crisis the magnitude of which threatens the very existence of the organization, even fewer would seriously consider bringing in an external consultant to help them identify and face the brutal facts. In some ways they're the optimists in the prisoner of war camp alongside James Stockdale wishing for Christmas, then Easter, then Thanksgiving, then Christmas, and in the end their organizational fate is the same as those prisoners of war. They die of a broken organizational heart. They lack the courage to face the brutal facts, the will to cling to a faith that they will prevail, and perhaps most importantly, they are paralyzed by their fear of taking a look in the organizational mirror. In those organizations everyone loses. The staff, volunteers, donors, funding partners, and the people served through the organization;'s programs and services.

Sadly, by the time some of those organizations respond to the urgency of the crisis, they hang on the precipice between organizational demise and the hope of a better future. Sometimes, those that do find themselves in that critical a situation are almost beyond the point of no return.

Others like one nonprofit organization I'm familiar with choose to turn a blind eye to the brutal facts. The Board of Directors for this client had conducted a extensive and far reaching 360 evaluation on the Executive Director in conjunction with a decision related to extending the Executive Director's 5 year term which was about to expire. The evaluation process involved soliciting input from over 60 people which in and of itself was somewhat odd. When the results were tabulated, the outcome was not pretty. There were major issues identified with the management style of the Executive Director. The Executive of the Board received the results of the evaluation but chose to keep the results to themselves providing a sanitized executive summary to the full Board. The sanitized version indicated that no major issues had surfaced and the recommendation of the Executive to the Board was that the Executive Director be reappointed for a second 5 year term. As some Board members began to question the process, and request more specifics related to the evaluation, they were effectively silenced and marginalized. While the vote to extend the term of the Executive Director passed it was not unanimous.

Not long after the appointment issues surfaced among the Executive Leadership Team. A major new initiative, which the

Executive Director had not kept the Board apprised of, went sideways in a big way. The Board became aware and held a special meeting and invited the Executive Director and two members of the Executive Management Team to the meeting. In doing so, they violated their governance protocol of having only one employee, that being the Executive Director. The minute the Board got involved in dealing directly with staff, they compromised the governance role and authority.

The outcome of that meeting was the decision to place one of the Executive Management Team members on probation, in effect holding her responsible for the project, in spite of the fact that final approval had come in a conference call initiated by the Executive Director which the Executive Management Team member was on vacation. The terms of the probation stipulated that a meeting between the individual, the Executive Director and the VP of Human Resources on the Board occur at 30, 60, and 90 day intervals to determine the individuals level of compliance. Those dates came and went and no meetings ever occurred. Upon receiving the terms of the probation, the individual had emailed the Chair of the Board requesting clarification as to what "compliance" would look like in terms of behaviour change. The Chair of the Board never responded to that email. After the Board appointed dates had passed with no meetings take place as stipulated in the terms of the probation, the individual sent the entire Board a letter inquiring as to when she might expect a response to her original email to the Board Chair, and when the Board mandated meetings might take place. Within short order she received a formal letter from the Board indicating that when the Board had placed her on probation they really had no plan in place as to what they intended outcomes might be, so it was unfair to hold the Executive Director and VP of Human Resources responsible to follow through on those meetings. They begged forgiveness and hoped that would be sufficient. The Executive Management Team member took that letter to a lawyer specializing in employment law and a protracted severance process ensued. All because the Board chose to ignore, deny, and refute the brutal facts.

Ironically the individual's successor in that role went through a similar experience with the Executive Director, only much worse. The Board was again made aware of the issues and chose again to avoid taking the look in the organizational mirror and that individual also transitioned out with the help of a lawyer. I wish this was fable, but it's not and it's not unique to just this organization. This happens with greater regularity in nonprofits that what you might expect. That being the case, all is not lost. There are anomalies if you will, stories like Kenaston where occasionally a Board stands up, demonstrates courage and does the right thing. So read on!

Chapter 9
Kenaston House - Right People

Doug, Heather, and Mark met shortly after the Board meeting to initiate the process of implementing some of the recommendations contained in Tim's report related to staffing transitions. It was agreed that the first order of business was to arrange a meeting with Kenaston's legal counsel to determine how best to proceed in a manner that would be fair to the staff being transitioned out and ensure that any actions taken by the Board would be in compliance with labour laws. Given the importance of that meeting they called the law firm and an appointment was set up for the following week.

The second order of business involved securing the services of an executive employment agency experienced working with nonprofit organizations like Kenaston. Doug had some connections and offered to initiate contact with one agency they were all familiar with and arrange a meeting subsequent to their meeting with the lawyer.

The initial meeting with the lawyer was both informative and extremely helpful as he outlined for them their legal responsibilities in transitioning Brad out of his role with the organization. Given that he was going to be off on medical leave, that complicated the exit strategy for Brad. The lawyer advised that the Board inform Brad they would be negotiating an exit strategy for Brad given the results of the consulting process they had been engaged in. As difficult as it was to contemplate that, they knew that Brad was not the right person to fill the role of Executive Director. That was contributing greatly to his emotional, physical, and professional fatigue.

The meeting with the executive employment agency was equally informative and enlightening. Surprising would be another adjective to describe the experience. One of the first things the agency did was conduct a talent assessment of the Executive Management Team with Doug, Heather, and Mark. The process was designed to identify the strengths, qualities and attributes of each of the management team members and correlate those to the responsibilities and expectations associated with each position.

Several things emerged out of that process that coincided with Tim's finding in his consulting report. Brad, Karyn, and Mary were each identified as lacking the required skill set and competence for the roles they occupied in the organization. Corresponding with Tim's assessment, Jennifer was unquestionably the right person for the role she occupied and she stood out head and shoulders above every one of her colleagues on the management team. This was reassuring as they contemplated the actions the Board would have to undertake moving forward.

Perhaps the most surprising piece that emerged out of the talent assessment was the recognition that as much as Brad wasn't a good fit as the Executive Director, without question he possessed the required skill set and competency to be the Program Director for Kenaston House, a position he had held in another organization prior to joining Kenaston. Heather wondered aloud if perhaps Brad might be open to transition into the role of Program Director in a restructured Executive Management Team. The suggestion caught Doug and Mark off guard but as they reflected on it they began to see the merits of Heather's suggestion. As they talked about it in more detail, there was a growing sense that this was an option worth serious consideration. It would be less stressful for Brad, free him from the responsibilities he currently had, responsibilities he really wasn't good at, and would provide some organizational stability in the significant transition that was about to unfold. All of this was contingent on Brad being open to the suggestion, and a satisfactory legal opinion from the lawyer assuring them that such a move would in no way contravene labour laws or expose Kenaston to potential litigation. Doug was tasked to contact the lawyer and communicate back to Heather and Mark the lawyer's opinion given this change in plans. They agreed that the talent assessment process had been an invaluable and important first step in the process. They also confirmed that until such time as the Board had decided how best to address the potential new job transition for Brad and his response to that, they would wait to proceed on a formal recruiting process for a new Executive Director.

Doug's call to the lawyer was brief and to the point. The lawyer indicated that as long as Brad agreed to the change in roles, the Board was not in violation of any labour laws and would not expose the organization to any potential litigation. Doug immediately conveyed that information to Heather and Mark. They agreed that their idea of transitioning Brad into the role of Program Director required Board approval so Mark was asked to provide an outline of the idea to the Board via email and ask the Board for their feedback and input on the suggestion.

Board members were quick to respond. The overwhelming response was that Doug, Heather and Mark should engage Brad in conversation about the idea. Board members could see the merits in what was being proposed and agreed that Brad's skills were better suited to the Program Director role than Executive Director. A number of Board members were adamant that Brad be given all the time off he needed to fully recuperate so that when he returned to work he was ready and able to fulfill the requirements of the role and do so with a high degree of competence and excellence.

With the Board clearly supportive of this new proposal,

Doug arranged a meeting with Brad and invited Heather and Mark to join him. Doug informed Brad that the Board had a proposal they wanted to discuses with him so Brad arrived at the meeting aware that something was up but unsure what exactly had prompted the meeting.

Doug began by asking Brad how he was doing and how he was progressing with some of the supports the group health care provider had put in place. Brad indicated that he had seen a medical doctor and was also seeing a psychologist. Both of those resources had been instrumental in helping Brad gain greater understanding about his situation, behavioural patterns, and his coping mechanisms. They were encouraged by Brad's update.

Doug then proceeded to update Brad on the Board's activities in his absence, specifically engaging Tim's consulting services and the report coming out of that process. Doug, Heather, and Mark assured Brad that they valued him as a person and his contribution to Kenaston House. They acknowledged that what had surfaced in the report was that Brad's skills seemed to be better suited to a role other than Executive Director. They were adamant that they wanted to retain Brad as a long term member of the Executive Management Team and in their talent assessment they had determined that he would be a much better fit as the Program Director. There would be a slight adjustment to his salary but given his wealth of experience in that role prior to joining Kenaston House, and his familiarity with the organization they recognized the contribution he could make in that role. They also indicated they felt it would be less stressful for Brad and would better play to his strengths and passions. He would thrive as would Kenaston House.

Brad was relieved that he still had a job and was actually quite encouraged by the conversation. What was being proposed to him coincided with one of the things he had been learning about himself in his work with the psychologist. He was not an Executive Director! That wasn't his skill set, his passion, or his strength. The fact that he had spent five years in a role that he was ill-suited for had contributed significantly to his current emotional, physical, and psychological state. He shared with them what he had been learning about himself and indicated that he would be more than willing to transition into this role as he too felt it was a better fit for him. He was of course concerned about the impact on Karyn and wondered how a new Executive Director would feel about having him in the position of Program Director given that he had been the Executive Director. Doug assured him that the Board would handle those issues and he should focus on his own recovery so that he could return to work healthy as a significant contributing member of the Executive Management Team.

With Brad having agreed to accept a revised role with Kenaston House, Doug connected with the executive employment agency to initiate the process of recruiting and hiring a new Executive Director. This was going to be a critical piece in the unfolding puzzle at Kenaston. Getting this hire right was absolutely essential if Kenaston was to emerge from its current crisis to a stronger, more aligned position moving forward.

Doug, Heather, and Mark began talking about the process for dealing with the other staffing transitions related to Karyn and Mary. Navigating this process was going to be critical as well, not only from the standpoint of the optics of the transitions but also the day to day management of Kenaston. Given that Brad had agreed to take on the role of Program Director, and the recruitment process for a new Executive Director set to begin, there was an urgency to address some of Tim's other recommendations related to staffing transitions and address them in a way that was reasonable and fair to Karyn and Mary, yet decisive. This was not the time to waffle or vacillate in acting on the decisions that had been made. Doug would meet with both of them to inform them of the Board's decision and ensure that all of the necessary legal and financial documentation was in place so the process could be expedited and the transition smooth. In the interim, Jennifer would be asked to continue to be the point leader for the organization.

With the Executive Director recruiting process running concurrent with the other staffing developments, there was strong interest from a number of qualified applicants. Kenaston's reputation in the city made it a desirable place to work, at least from an outsider's perspective. Confident that there were enough suitable applicants, the agency began the process of short-listing the candidates and setting up interviews for those short-listed. Doug was thankful to have access to the resources of the employment agency to assist in this critical hiring process. There was little, if any margin for error. They had to get the right person to be the next Executive Director of Kenaston House.

Chapter 10
Your People - Your Core Asset

Would you enthusiastically rehire everyone on your team? Would you enthusiastically re-recruit every one of the volunteers who serve your organization? If your answer isn"t a resounding "yes" to both of those questions, you have a people issue in your organization. As you've observed in the story of Kenaston, having the wrong people in the wrong seat on the bus is a recipe for disaster. If the person in question functions in a supervisory role, they are frustrating the people working under their supervision, and you're not getting the most out of your people. Talent, productivity, and morale are all being wasted.

If you look at your Profit and Loss Statement, salaries probably constitute one of your organization's largest expenditures if not the largest expenditure. That being the case, your people are your core asset! Ensuring that you have the right person with the right skill set occupying the right "seat" in your organization, consistently executing the identified highest priority tasks with excellence is critical to growing your organization. Whether it's a for profit business or a nonprofit organization, your people are your biggest asset OR liability. And it's about more than having warm bodies with a heartbeat and a pulse. Even a pulse that beats passionately for your organization isn't enough. Without having the right people with the right skill set consistently executing the highest priority activities with excellence, your impact will be muted, team chemistry and effectiveness will be weakened, and you will spend a lot of time as an executive leader fighting fires and cleaning up messes. Therein lies a significant challenge for many nonprofit organizations. How do you recruit, hire, AND retain the right people?

Most often led by caring, compassionate people, be they employees or Board members, nonprofit organizations tend to have a more difficult time dealing with under performing employees, volunteers, and Board members. Usually these under performers are good people who are passionate about the organization's cause. Those responsible to manage and supervise them recognize, value, and appreciate those qualities. As a result they tend to lower the bar when it comes to job performance and accountability. When it comes to balanced measuring of productivity and people, the business world tends to focus predominantly on the productivity metric whereas nonprofits tend to focus primarily on the people metric. Both are wrong. As Jim Collins' research proved, the truly great companies focus on both productivity and people and do so in a disciplined, consistent, and persistent manner.

So what are the key ingredients to ensuring your organization has the right people in the right seats doing the right things right?

Core Values

Core values are the handful of rules and boundaries that define and shape your organization's culture, norms, and behaviors. Once established they won't change much over time. They outline what is acceptable as well as what is unacceptable in terms of organizational conduct, attitudes, and actions. Typically organizations don't think about core values when reflecting on the people who make the organization run but in one sense everything rises and falls on your organization's core values and having people on your team who not only embrace your core values but consistently live them out.

While some organizations have identified core values, often they are aspirational values - values they aspire to live out. Rarely do they monitor and measure how they're doing in terms of living out those core values. A better approach to identify core values is to articulate the core values currently alive in the organization, those norms and practises consistently evidenced in the lives of people already working within the organization. In some ways it's a very different way of identifying core values, but at the same time the process of monitoring and measuring core values is expedited when the focus is on articulating existing core values rather than aspirational values. That's not to say that you won't still identify some aspirational values, but they won't constitute the sum total of your core values or even the majority of your core values.

Bringing this conversation back to the people in your organization, having people in your organization who not only embrace your core values but consistently live them out gives credibility and power to your values. They are more than just words in a planning or marketing document. Those core values begin to shape and dictate what you do and how you do it. They define what's acceptable and what's unacceptable in terms of how you relate as a staff team, how you relate to the beneficiaries you serve, how you conduct yourself in relationships with donors and partner agencies.

Which begs a very important question. How would you know if what you've identified as your organization's core values really constitute core values? You'll know it's a core value when you're prepared to fire a staff person, volunteer or Board member who consistently fails or refuses to live out the core value. That may sound a bit drastic or perhaps harsh, but reflect on that for a moment. If it's really a core value, then it ought to be a non-negotiable in terms of your expectations of staff, Board, and volunteers. Where you see an individual who isn't consistent in living out one of your core values, it would be reasonable to expect their direct supervisor to spend time coaching that individual to help them more consistently live out the core value. If that individual is either unable to unwilling to consistently live out that core value it would be reasonable to terminate them from their role in the organization. To tolerate consistent noncompliance with one or more of the core values, devalues the core values and indicates to everyone else in the organization that they are something less than "core" values.

In order for your core values to be a significant, active, living force in your organization they must also be modelled and lived out by the Executive Leadership Team AND the Board of Directors. A failure to model the core values by the key leaders of any organization completely undermines the core values throughout the rest of the organization rendering them useless in terms of shaping organizational culture, behaviour, and norms.

I led a nonprofit organization through the process of articulating their core values. As they identified the organization's core values one thing became very clear. The Executive Director did not model and live out several of the core values. The Board of Directors all knew it and they knew that if the core values were going to impact their direction moving forward they would have to deal with the Executive Director. The person you met in public was very different than the person you met in the office or the Board room. Since one of their values was authenticity, they met with the Executive Director and confronted him on the gaps they saw between the identified core values and his behaviour in the exercise of his duties in the organization. They put in place an external coaching process to help him address some of the inconsistencies and issues they not only observed but had experienced personally. What became clear was that the Executive Director was unwilling to do the hard work required to more consistently live out the core values. The Board asked for an in camera meeting with me where we discussed their options. They knew what they had to do but that didn't make the decision any easier. The Board was comprised of caring people and they were concerned about how a decision to terminate him would impact the Executive Director's family. Some on the Board were so impacted by that they were prepared to do nothing and continue on status quo. Several others on the Board were adamant the Board needed to do the right (and hard) thing and terminate the Executive Director. I concurred with that perspective and challenged them to err on the side of generosity in their severance package, which they did. They recognized that they would have to answer some equally difficult questions from stakeholders who only encountered the public persona of the Executive Director but the Board stood firm with its decision. They did pay a price for their decision. Some donors cut off their support. Some volunteers stopped volunteering but many of the existing staff cheered on the Board for having the courage to make the tough decision. That's often the way it is - the right decisions are the tough decisions and the Board had the courage to do what was right even if it was hard.

What difference would it make in your organization if all of your people lived out your core values? What kind of a difference would it make if you placed such a high priority on your core values that you incorporated your core values into your employee performance review process and then terminated those employees who consistently failed or refused to live into and live out your core values? What difference would it make if you required not only your staff but your volunteers AND your Board to consistently live out your core values? The fact that they're volunteers ought to have no bearing on your expectations of them when it comes to living out the core values.

Don't your beneficiaries deserve at least that? I can imagine some resistance to this notion. "We might lose some volunteers or board members! What will we do then?" Ponder this. If an individual would stop volunteering because you expected them to live out your organization's core values, how much help were they in the first place? If they're not committed to living out your core values on a consistent basis, do you really want them representing your organization? There's no doubt these are tough questions, but they help determine whether or not your values are really "core".

Which raises another important point. What do you do when you have someone who is profoundly competent in the exercise of their duties within the organization but who doesn't live out the core values? Competence is no excuse to lower the standards in terms of the core values. I'm aware of one organization whose employee bonus structure is tied to performance metrics, goal accomplishment, AND living out the core values. It's entirely possible for an individual to perform well, achieve all of the identified personal and departmental goals but not live out the core values and therefore receive no bonus. You can rest assured in that organization, an employee would only miss one or two bonuses due to lack of compliance with the core values and a performance improvement plan would be implemented with clear expectations and measurable outcomes. Failure to meet the expectations of the performance improvement plan would result in termination.

For many nonprofit organizations the concept of such a disciplined focus and reinforcement of the core values represents a significant intellectual and emotional challenge requiring a radical paradigm shift. It goes against the notion of tolerance that is prevalent in so many nonprofit organizations. Those willing to embrace the challenge reap an exponential benefit internally within the organization, externally in the delivery of programs and services, and in their relationships with donors and funding agencies. What adds power and credibility to your core values is the endless stream of stories of people within your organization who consistently live out the core values. Organizational credibility skyrockets and along with that increased support.

Core Purpose

Beyond skill set and living out the Core Values, it's critical to have people involved in your organization who share a deep and passionate commitment to your core purpose. Core purpose answers the question, "Why?" Why do you do what you do? What is it that keeps you going on the days when funding and volunteers are in short supply? What would your community miss if your organization ceased to exist?

How you answer those questions helps frame your core purpose, your raison d'etre if you will. The clearer you can be on your core purpose and incorporate that into your recruiting and hiring process, the more likely you are to attract people who share your organization's core purpose, who want the same things your organization wants. Clarity around core purpose and regular reinforcement of the core purpose within your organization helps individuals connect at a heart level with what your organization is fundamentally about. That applies to staff, volunteers, donors, and funding agencies. Your core purpose needs to capture either one word or one idea. Many nonprofit organizations have flowery, expansive mission or vision statements. They make great copy but they're far too complex and lengthy for people to remember. When it comes to your core purpose, less is more! The more succinct you are in outlining your core purpose, the greater the likelihood that people will easily and quickly grab on to it. The greater the likelihood that they'll own it as their own!

As I worked with one client in developing their core purpose I asked if they had a mission statement. The prompt reply was "Yes we do!" My immediate question was, "What is it?" All eye contact was lost as individuals shifted their gaze to the floor. Not one person knew what the mission statement was! Finally one brave soul ventured, "Does anyone have the policy manual?" The Chair of the Board indicated she did and she retrieved the said mission statement from her policy manual and handed it to me. I read the lengthy, flowery mission statement aloud for the group. It sounded so good, but not one of their executive leadership team knew what it was! When I had finished reading, one astute Board member offered a sarcastic, tongue in cheek "Wow, I'm inspired." I know that experience is not unique to that organization. The same could be said of many nonprofit organizations.

Once you get succinct clarity on your core purpose it becomes the compelling story you tell over and over again to every person you meet! As you tell and retell the story it attracts people to your organization - staff, volunteers, donors, funding agencies, and partner organizations. It's a story that every staff member ought to be able to recite verbatim because it's been so ingrained in them, it so impacts every aspect of who you are as an organization, what you're about, and what you do!

Core Competencies

Once you have clarity around your core values and core purpose, it's important to articulate your core competencies. Core competencies have three components. They're not easy for other organizations or agencies to replicate of copy, they are reflected in the majority, if not all of your programs and services, and they provide a maximum benefit and impact for the people who access those programs and services.

Engaging the exercise of articulating the organization's core competencies is difficult for many nonprofits. Difficult in that many are motivated by a sense of humility that sees this exercise as self-effacing and almost arrogant. But the second reason it's difficult is that in articulating what your organization is good at, you must also name those things that you're not good at. Invariably some of the things an organization is not good at consume a significant amount of organizational resources in terms of time and money! Often some of those programs and services have been in place for an extended period of time and people within the organization display a territorial protectionism which silences even the most generic conversation as to whether or not the organization should continue to engage that program or service. As a result, valuable resources are deployed to activities that ultimately don't fit the organizational core values, core purpose, or core competencies. Having identified those things the organization is NOT good at, now forces an even more difficult conversation. Why should the organization keep doing those things which it has recognized it's not good at? The implicit answer is, "It shouldn't!" But the decision to stop doing some of the things the organization has been doing for a long time is never made without great courage on the part of the executive leadership team and some fallout is usually unavoidable.

Right People Right Seats

Clarity on Core Values, Core Purpose, and Core Competencies dramatically increases the likelihood that you will attract the right people to staff your organization, serve as volunteers, and Board members. Recruiting, hiring, and retaining people who fit the core of what your organization is about is a non-negotiable if you want to see your organization thrive and grow. Competence ranks lower down the list than core values and core purpose. Make no mistake about it, competency is an indispensable ingredient, but it's possible to be highly competent but not fit with the core values and core purpose of the organization. Core Values and Core Purpose always trump competency when it comes to recruiting, hiring and retaining the right people for your organization. Someone who fully embraces and lives out your Core Values and Core Purpose will usually have an inherent openness to personal development and their competency can be developed. There reverse is not always the case. When you are able to find a competent person who lives out your core values, core purpose and core competencies the potential for positive impact in the organization increases exponentially. Ideally that' the kind of people you want in your organization. That's why the recruiting and hiring process is so critical. Your people are your Core Asset.

Before you can hire the right people, you need to identify the right staff positions in the organization. What functions in your organization need to be filled by a staff person as compared to a volunteer? Do each of those functions require a separate individual to be responsible for the function or can one individual be responsible for multiple functions? Identifying the right positions in your organization is another critical piece. The danger with nonprofits is that one person will be tasked with more responsibilities and functions than what they can reasonably manage efficiently. Most often those decisions are driven by economic realities but the cost savings are imaginary due to reduced efficiencies. Having said that, sometimes several functions can quite naturally be grouped together with one person responsible without in any way compromising organizational efficiencies or individual job performance. Once the correct staff positions have been identified then the required skill set and competencies can be outlined to ensure that you have the right person who lives the core values, embraces the core purpose, AND has the right skill set and competencies matched to the role within the organization. Beyond that, the individual must have unmistakable clarity on how their particular role and function impacts the overall direction of the organization. They ought to be able to answer the question, "How does what I do help us get to where we want to go?"

Chapter 11
Kenaston House - Finding the Right Person

Driven by the profound and unwavering realization that getting the right person with the right skill set who embraced the core values, core purpose, and core competencies of Kenaston House, the recruiting and hiring process went ahead with intentionality and focus yielding several highly qualified candidates who were appropriately short-listed. With the help of the employment agency, interviews were set up with the three leading candidates. Doug, Heather, and Mark were involved in the interview process to ensure that the Board had significant input into the process. Once they had narrowed the search down to one candidate they would then arrange for that individual to meet with the entire Board.

The employment agency suggested that the Board employ the Topgrading methodology in the interview process. While there was a cost involved in utilizing that process, the employment agency assured the Board that the return on investment would far exceed the associated fees given that it would dramatically increase the level of certainty and fit related to the next Executive Director. The Board agreed that this was an expense worth incurring given the minimal margin for error in the hiring process.

As they interviewed the three candidates, one immediately rose to the top of everyone's list. Donna Murphy had a long track record of leading nonprofit organizations comparable to Kenaston House in terms of budget, size of staff, and community profile. She had successfully led and developed not only those organizations but also the management teams of each organization. This was borne out by the Topgrading methodology which incorporated rigorous screening mechanisms designed to increase the likelihood of hiring the right person with the right skill set for the job. One of the intriguing aspects of the Topgrading process was that Donna contacted her own references and informed them they would be receiving a call from one of the interviewers requesting a reference check. As the references were contacted, each of them corroborated what the interviewers had heard and experienced from Donna in the interview process. As they debriefed after the interview, and the reference check process concluded they were unanimous that Donna should meet the entire Board in the hope that the Board would concur with their assessment and offer her the position of Executive Director.

When the Board met with Donna, they quickly reached the same conclusions as Doug, Heather and Mark following their interview with Donna. The Board went into significant detail informing Donna of what had transpired leading up to the recruiting, interview and hiring process. They wanted her to be as informed as possible so that there were fewer surprises when she actually came on Board.

Several of the issues they went into more detail on related to the results coming out of Tim Kennedy's consulting report. It was important that she be aware of the significant challenges within the Executive Management Team. They informed her of Brad's medical leave and their conversations related to Brad transitioning into the role of Program Director. They wanted to ensure she would be okay working with Brad in this new role, given the fact that he had been the Executive Director. Donna indicated that she would have no issue with that and would work quickly to establish clear guidelines and parameters for the working relationship.

The Board also informed Donna that one of her first tasks would be to hire a new Volunteer Coordinator given that both Karyn and Mary would be terminated prior to Donna assuming the role of Executive Director. Given Donna's connections in the city, she indicated she had several candidates that she thought would not only have the necessary skill set but would also fit the culture they were trying to create and foster at Kenaston.

The final topic of conversation was introduced as a non-negotiable by the Board. That was the matter of implementing the recommended planning process outlined in Tim's report. The Board wanted to make sure that Donna fully embraced the planning process and would become the champion for that process within the Executive Management Team and the staff as a whole. Donna was familiar with Tim and his work and she indicated that if the Board hadn't brought up the subject of a planning process, she would have brought it up and it would have been a non-negotiable for her as well. What was emerging was an unprecedented synergy and alignment between the Board and Donna. Both sides felt that there was a strong relational foundation upon which a healthy, productive working relationship could be built.

Donna was excused from the meeting but told not to leave the building. The Board wanted to make a decision relative to offering her the position and indicated they would notify her when they had made their decision. Mark made a motion that Donna be offered the position and Heather quickly seconded the motion. There was a brief discussion and Doug called for a vote. It was unanimous and the entire process took less than 5 minutes! Donna was called in and informed of the Board decision. She accepted their offer on the spot and they began working out the logistics of a start date and other employment particulars. They also indicated that they would be meeting with Karyn and Mary the next day to inform them of the Board's decision to move in a different direction related to their employment with Kenaston. They would also meet with

Jennifer to inform her of the staffing transitions that were un-folding and assure her of her long term status as a key member of the Executive Management Team. Everyone left the meeting with a sense of hope and optimism, confident that they had indeed found the right person to lead Kenaston into the next phase of its organizational life.

Doug and Heather immediately made arrangements with Karyn and Mary to meet with them separately the following day. Neither of them were looking forward to the meetings but they knew that for the sake of everyone involved, the meetings needed to take place sooner rather than later. They also arranged to meet with Jennifer to update her on all that had transpired.

The individual meetings with Karyn and Mary went as well as could be expected. They were informed that as a result of the consulting process the Board had initiated with Tim, there was a need to make some significant changes in terms of the management team composition and structure. Those changes had direct implications for each of them which were outlined for them. While the Board had agreed to be generous in the severance packages they offered each of them, the shock and pain was unavoidable.

Following the more difficult meetings with Karyn and Mary, Doug and Heather spent considerable time with Jennifer, informing her of the Board decisions and talking about the path moving forward. While Jennifer felt sad for Karyn and Mary, she knew it was the right move and also affirmed the transition of Brad from Executive Director to Program Director. As Doug and Heather briefed her on Donna's appointment, Jennifer's excitement was noticeable. She had heard about Donna and everything she had heard gave her reason to hope again! Finally there would be a strong Executive Director with leadership skills to provide oversight and direction to the organization. For the first time in a long time she had hope that Kenaston could be much more intentional and strategic in meeting the needs of its existing beneficiaries and actually grow their program and service deliver options moving forward. As she reflected back on all that had transpired in a short period of time, she was incredibly thankful that she had risked being as open with the Board as she had been. In hindsight, it had proven to be instrumental to not only addressing the current crisis but also setting a new direction moving into the future, a direction which would be sustainable.

With Donna's hiring confirmed along with a start date, the Board informed the rest of the staff. While there was sadness surrounding the departure of Karyn and Mary, there was a sense of excitement around Donna's appointment. There was also a general sense of affirmation related to Brad's revised role with the organization. Most staff who'd been there for a while knew that Brad was better suited to be the Program Director than the Executive Director and they were genuinely happy for him, and looked forward to working with him in his new role.

One of Donna's first orders of business was to conduct a facility wide staff meeting. No one could remember the last time there had been such a meeting. What because evident very quickly was that Donna was a leader. She commanded respect. She didn't demand it - she commanded it. A subtle but very important difference. There was no doubt she had conducted these kinds of meetings before and had a level of expertise and proficiency that was impressive. It made you want to follow her! She was a good communicator who clearly had a plan as to what her expectations were, what the staff could expect from her, and how things were going to work under her watch as Executive Director. What was also striking was the immediate chemistry between Jennifer and Donna, something which did not go unnoticed by the staff. It was like they had worked together for years! In the midst of all the transition taking place, in an odd way, that chemistry was a huge stabilizing factor on the entire staff team. That kind of chemistry had never existed between Brad and Jennifer. As Jennifer and Donna began working together, that chemistry continued to grow as did their productivity. For the first time in her tenure at Kenaston, Jennifer felt like she had an ally occupying the Executive Director's office! Rather than dreading coming into work, work was now a place where she felt incredibly alive, invigorated, and energized.

Donna immediately began the task of hiring a new Volunteer Coordinator. Given her extensive connections in the city, news of her appointment as the Executive Director of Kenaston House spread quickly and along with that the number of people contacting her about the vacant position. Given her track record as a leader, there were a host of qualified and very competent people who wanted to come work with her at Kenaston. Not surprisingly, they shared the kinds of core values that had endeared Donna to the Board and would become the values that were monitored, measured, and lived out in Kenaston moving forward. Those values were already present in people like Jennifer but the priority of those values would be championed, modelled and celebrated by Donna and the rest of the Executive Management Team.

As Donna reviewed the applications for the vacant Volunteer Coordinator position, Jeff Miller's resume immediately rose to the top of the pile. Donna was familiar with Jeff and his work in another organization in the city and was impressed with his character and his competence in the role. He had a proven track record of recruiting quality volunteers, coordinating volunteer schedules and developing a team chemistry among the volunteers he worked with. The volunteers who worked for him all spoke well of him and actually were some of his best recruiters, going out and recruiting their friends because of how good an experience they had volunteering under Jeff's leadership. Jeff had also made significant inroads with several large companies who encouraged their staff to volunteer with organizations Jeff was associated with as a way of giving back to the community. Their employees always came back with impassioned stories of their volunteer experiences. As Donna interviewed Jeff, it became clear to her and to Jeff that this could be a good fit for him and for Kenaston. Donna brought Jennifer into one of her meetings with Jeff which caught Jennifer completely by surprise. She had never experienced that before but it was clear that Donna's management style was inclusive, wanting to make sure that not only did she have a good feeling about Jeff, but that Jennifer shared it as well. This was about building a strong, cohesive, and aligned Executive Management Team who not only were competent, lived the core values, but enjoyed working together as a team! After talking with Jennifer, Donna offered Jeff the position of Volunteer Coordinator which he accepted and she set out to address the next priority - meeting with Brad.

Recognizing that Brad was on medical leave, Donna contacted him and asked him is he would be open to having lunch with her. He agreed and they arranged to meet at the same restaurant where Brad had broken the news to Doug about what was really going on at Kenaston. While Brad knew about Donna, he'd never really talked with her at any great length so he wasn't sure what to expect. One of the first things he noticed about her was how much she made him feel at ease. She wasn't threatened or intimidated by him given the fact that he had previously held the position of Executive Director. She was also incredibly caring, focusing in on his physical, emotional, and psychological well-being. She took great interest in his own recovery process and how this was all impacting him personally as well as his family. Like Jennifer, Brad too was surprised by Donna. She was not what he had expected. Within the first 20 minutes of conversation, he knew he would have no problem working for her, and she felt the same. Donna shared some general ideas she had about the direction moving forward at Kenaston but she assured Brad that he should take whatever time he needed to get well, so that when he returned he could engage his new role refreshed and invigorated as a key member of the Executive Management Team. Brad indicated that Doug's conversation with him suggesting a change in role within Kenaston had actually been a huge relief and a significant factor in the speed of his own recovery. He felt as if a huge weight had been lifted off his shoulders. His psychologist and medical doctor had indicated that he would probably be ready to return to work within a month given some of the transitions that had taken place and the support he had been receiving through his engagement with the professionals working with him in the process. Donna suggested that Brad return to work on a gradual basis for the first several weeks to monitor his ability to handle the revised duties and responsibilities.

With the restructured Executive Management Team falling into place, Donna met with Doug and Tim Kennedy to talk about the consulting report and develop a timeline for implementing the planning process. She had read Tim's report several times and wasn't surprised or challenged by anything Tim had outlined in it. It was clear there were some challenges but Donna had seen this script played out before so it wasn't new to her. She found it inspiring and energizing! She could hardly wait to embark on the planning adventure and that's exactly how she viewed it - an adventure!

As the three of them talked about the process and the timeline, the sense of alignment and synergy was palpable. There was no doubt they were all tracking in the same direction, not because one or more of them were compliant. Quite the contrary. They were all strong personalities and they weren't afraid to state their opinion and challenge someone else's opinion. But they were respectful in how they did that and were as open to receive challenge as they were to give it! One thing they all agreed on was that the process could not commence until Brad was back full time in his role as Program Director. The entire Executive Management Team needed to be fully engaged in this process along with the Board so they set a date 6 weeks out to give Brad time to transition back in. This also provided Donna valuable time to orient herself more fully with the inner workings of Kenaston as well as give Jeff a chance to get somewhat incorporated into the day-to-day operations of the organization. Tim and Donna agreed to meet weekly to review her discoveries and perspectives as she immersed herself in the role as well as finalize the specifics of what the planning process would look like.

As Doug reflected on all that had transpired in a relatively short period of time, and the significant impact of Brad's authentic self-disclosure, the Board's courageous decisions, and Donna's immediate positive leadership impact at Kenaston, he was reminded of one thing Tim told him during their lunch meeting to review the Tim's report. Tim called it the "Power of One" effect. He explained it this way. All it takes for an organizational system to move towards greater health and functioning is for one person to step back from that organizational system, take a look back at the system from the perspective of an outsider and then change the way they relate back to that system. As Doug reflected back on the process, he could see a number of "Power of One" decision that had taken place. He began to list them - the meeting with Brad, the meeting with the Board, the decision to contract Tim, the decision to re-position Brad within the organization, the decision to implement all of Tim's recommendations, the decision to terminate Karyn and Mary, the decision to hire Donna, Donna's management style and the impact already on the organization.

Each of those meetings and decisions had a "Power of One" impact on Kenaston. In one way or another each represented a radical departure from the status quo. Now with Donna and Jeff coming in as a complete outsiders they would bring a fresh perspective that Doug knew was bound to challenge some of those who had been around for a while. He knew that wasn't a bad thing for Kenaston. Deep down he believed that in order for the organization to survive, that's exactly what they needed. He was willing to be the "Power of One" at the Board level to ensure that Donna had the governance support she needed to facilitate the changes and growth Kenaston so desperately needed. As chaotic as the last 6 weeks had been, he was like a horse ready to race! Let's get on with this already! In some ways the worst was over. That didn't mean there wouldn't be challenges ahead, but they had a team that was aligned and ready to meet those challenges ,and address them in proactive and collaborative ways.

Chapter 12
Kenaston House - Strategic Thinking

With Donna settling into a routine 6 weeks into the job, Jeff transitioning in, and Brad getting back up to full speed the time was right to begin the planning process outlined by Tim Kennedy in his report to the Board. Donna had set aside two days for the Board and Executive Management Team to engage the strategic thinking and execution planning process. This was a new process for everyone currently associated with Kenaston. Each of them had their own idea as to what a strategic planning process would look like. They had heard horror stories of other organizations who had engaged a similar process, which ended up having little impact on the long term direction of the organization or the day to day management of it. No one was quite sure if this kind of process had ever been engaged before in the history of Kenaston House. While there were a lot of unknowns in terms of what the process would look like and what the outcomes would be, there was an air of cautious anticipation as they gathered together in an offsite location to focus intentionally on the big picture framework that would serve to guide Kenaston moving forward. Something about this process seemed different than what they had heard about in other organizations. Tim has specifically requested that the Executive Management Team and the Board participate in this process together. Since the Board was responsible for the strategic direction of the organization as a part of their governance mandate, and the Executive Management Team was responsible for the implementation and execution of the strategic direction, both groups needed to be at the table for the strategic thinking process. This would prove critical to the effectiveness of the process and its positive impact on Kenaston moving forward.

People - The Core

Since the group had never been together in this format, Tim began with an icebreaker which really served to help them get to know each other and lighten the mood. Recognizing that people naturally sit with people they know and feel comfortable with, he had them all stand up against a wall - Board members on one wall and Executive Management Team on the opposite wall. Then he had each group number off 1 through 3 and instructed them to sit at the table that corresponded with their number. He wanted each table to have a mix of Board members and staff for the interaction and discussions that would take place over the course of the next two days. He knew it would push them out of their comfort zones but the next two days were going to be a stretching experience so no better time to start the stretching process than right at the beginning! If they couldn't handle this amount of stretching, the rest of the process would really test their mettle.

The first exercise Tim led the team through was an activity he called a "Mission to Mars." Some of them immediately wondered how this activity would in any way help Kenaston as an organization moving forward. The instructions were simple. Imagine that you're going to take five people with you to Mars. Pick those who best represent and embody what Kenaston stands for as an organization to start a new division of Kenaston House. Which 5 people currently a part of Kenaston would you take with you and what one characteristic do each of them manifest that in your opinion exemplifies what Kenaston is about? They set to work individually identifying their team of 5 and the character qualities each of them possessed. When Tim called them back together as a group he instructed them to start sharing their individual lists around their table. Something remarkable occurred as they starting comparing lists. Their lists were surprisingly similar. In fact, there were some names that appeared on everyone's list around the table! To say they were surprised at what this simple exercise had already begun to generate in terms of energy and enthusiasm would not be an understatement. Each table was tasked to agree on their five person list. Once they'd had sufficient time to compare lists around their tables, Tim moved to the white Board and asked each table to identify their five person team. As names were mentioned Tim wrote them on the whiteboard. You could hear the whispering at other tables as one by one Tim made his way around until each table had provided their list. The energy in the room was palpable. They were surprised at how similar their lists were, and that without any collaboration between the groups! Tim also listed the character quality that each person embodied.

Having recorded the responses from each group, Tim said, "You've just begun to identify the Core Values that are already alive and active within Kenaston House!" There was a "Duh, of course!" kind of look on many faces in the room! They had never ever talked about it as a group, yet this seemingly simple exercise had helped them identify core values that already shaped who they were as an organization, how they behaved and went about their work .

As they looked at the list of Core Values there was another realization that surfaced. There were employees who didn't embody the core values. Tim said, "You'll know these are really core values when you're prepared to fire an offender regardless of their position in the organization for their failure to consistently live out these core values." You could have heard a pin drop, but as the initial impact of Tim's statement had time to sink in, it made sense. As they reflected on some of the developments in the months leading up to this 2 day planning event, they realized that Karyn and Mary didn't embody them either. Putting that into practise and consistently following through on it would be the challenge. Tim reminded them of one critical reality. These core values were going to shape not only how they treated residents in the facility but also how they treated each other as staff colleagues, how they treated donors, funding partners, suppliers, and others who connected with Kenaston.

The core values they identified and agreed to embrace were celebration, compassion, dignity, excellence, and passion. They were going to affirm and celebrate growth and progress as they saw it in the residents in the facility as well as within the staff team. They were going to treat people with compassion recognizing that each one of them had their own "story." That would apply to residents and staff colleagues. They recognized that no matter how difficult the residents' current life situation was and the challenges each of them had coping with their life situation they still deserved to be treated with respect and dignity. They also affirmed that excellence had to be the new "normal" in terms of how everyone within Kenaston approached their role within the organization. It couldn't be just the few standouts who modelled and embodied this. It had to be everyone within the organization! Probably the core value that was most consistently lived out was passion. The vast majority of the staff were there because they were passionate about the work they were engaged in and they would continue to vigorously wave the passion flag. Those who didn't share the passion for what they did would either catch the "virus" or move on from Kenaston House.

While some had wondered how a seemingly disjointed and esoteric exercise could ever help them as a leadership team, they had living proof that Tim's exercise had brought them to a significant starting point in framing and implementing a new organizational culture. Communicating, reinforcing, living out, and celebrating those values would require persistent modelling and diligence from each of them as the executive leaders of Kenaston.

Core Purpose - The Big "Why?"

Capitalizing on the energy created by the Mission to Mars exercise, Tim laid out the next exercise. Why do you do what you do? Why is it important? Why does it matter? What would this city lose if Kenaston House didn't exist? What was the passion that drove Nancy Watson to start Kenaston House over 30 years ago? He again had them work in groups and provided a simple worksheet to frame their work and guide their discussion. The worksheet involved them asking the same two questions multiple times - Why does it matter? Why is it important? Some wondered why they had to ask the same questions more than once? Wasn't once enough? But as they followed Tim's lead, they realized that what happened as they revisited the same questions and continued to refine their answers, they were refining and getting greater clarity related to their Core Purpose as an organization. As Tim observed their interaction around the tables, he noticed the energy continuing to build. There was passion and excitement as they dialogued and debated among themselves. At some tables the debate was spirited and at points even intense.

As Tim called them back together into the larger group and began recording the results of the work in the individual groups on the flip chart, there was an audible wow that emerged from the group as a whole! Without any collaboration between groups the same themes were emerging from each of the groups. The synergy and growing sense of alignment was astounding. Equally surprising was the latent alignment already present within the group, alignment that had never been maximized to more intentionally focus their energies as a team or for that matter, the organizational direction.

Once Tim had the themes recorded on the flip chart they began to synthesize the data into a one phrase strategy that captured the essence of some of the dominant themes. The conversation was spirited and focused. There were several dominant themes which rose to the top of the list. They acknowledged that most of their residents had little sense of hope that life could be anything other than what they knew it to be. It was like they were doomed to their current reality. As much as they wanted something different they had no confidence that they could ever realize it. The other theme that emerged was the staff's passionate belief that change was possible. Those two themes helped them crystallize their Core Purpose into a clear, concise, memorable statement - "Giving Hope - Transforming Lives" As Tim wrote it on the flip chart there was a collective sense of "Yes, That's It!" Each one of them knew that was what motivated them to get up in the morning and give their all to the work they did at Kenaston House.

BHAG - Big Hairy Audacious Goal

With the positive energy continuing to build and pulsate throughout the group, Tim pressed on! "Let's start dreaming If you think 10-15 years down the road, what's your dream for Kenaston? Where do you want to be at as an organization? What will Kenaston look like? What programs and services will you deliver?" He called it a BHAG - a big hairy audacious goal. This was a term none of them had heard before but they certainly got the concept. He gave them some simple instructions focused around some framing questions. What are you passionate about? What do you do better than anybody else in the city? What are the people and financial resources you have at your disposal? Given your responses to those three questions, what's your dream for Kenaston 10-15 years down the road?

Rather than having them work in smaller groups, Tim had them engage this exercise as a whole group. They knew they were passionate about helping women with episodic and chronic homelessness caused in large part because of some mental health challenges. They also knew they were passionate about seeing these women move from living in a shelter environment to living independently with an enhanced ability to cope with their mental health challenges. They acknowledged that this was their contribution to the city and whatever their current challenges were, they still delivered those services better than any other agency in the city! As they evaluated their people and financial resources, they realized they had a few employees who were shining stars. They had credibility in the city with government departments, other agencies and the public in general.

After some passionate and engaged interaction, Brenda, one of the case managers offered this comment. "We're really good at providing emergency shelter and first stage housing for women with mental health challenges but there's nobody that is really set up to provide second stage housing for these women. If we get a woman who does really well in our apartment unit, where does she go from there? There's no other facility we can transition her to where we're confident that she's going to have the supports she needs to live independently." Every head in the room nodded in agreement. She continued, "There's that property next door that is really run down. What if we bought that property with the idea of developing a second stage housing complex there? There's nothing like that in the city now and I'm sure we could get the funding for it because there's a huge need for that! We're ideally positioned to be the agency who provides that level of service in the city!" The energy in the room continued to build. Most of them were surprised at how much they had accomplished in the short time they had been together! Tim had seen this many times before so it was no surprise to him! As they continued to dream, they agreed Kenaston was the leading provider of emergency shelter and first stage housing for women in the city. They knew there was a need for second stage housing. Donna had been doodling, obviously working on something important. "I've got an idea for our BHAG. Kenaston House will be the primary provider of emergency shelter, first, and second stage housing for women with mental health challenges in our city with a legacy of 'success' stories!" There was an audible gasp of excitement that reverberated through the group! One by one Board members and staff alike responded with "I really like it!" Tim went around the room asking each person for their feedback and input into the BHAG. There was unanimous agreement and not because they were compliant "yes" people. Everyone of them agreed with it at a deep, visceral level. Each of them knew it would involve hard work and require significant changes but they were energized at the thought of working toward that goal!

Having allowed sufficient time for discussion, Tim posed a two-part question, "How will you measure your progress towards your goal? How will you know when you've reached that goal?" That led to an important conversation about metrics. Doug Hampton posed a very interesting question, "What are the metrics we focus on now?" There was an awkward silence from the Executive Management Team. "The only thing we measure with any kind of consistency is how many people stay in our shelter." Doug followed with another question, "So do you track how many of your residents move from the shelter to the first stage apartment units?" Another pregnant, awkward pause. "No, we don't" Donna, new to the job asked another probing question, "In our case management, do we have a tangible case management plan for each person who registers in our shelter and each resident in the apartment units?" More awkward silence. "No we don't have that either." You could feel some of the life and energy being sucked out of the room which Tim quickly picked up on. "A key part of this process is not so much about finding the right answers. It's about asking the right questions. You are asking the right questions and while you might not like the answers, that's okay! The questions you're raising are critical to helping shape your course of action moving forward. They're helping you identify some of the key issues you need to focus on as you seek to make your BHAG a reality. But let's keep moving!"

Core Beneficiary

Tim now shifted the focus to type of person Kenaston was best suited to reach and most focused on working with. He did this by introducing the concept of a Core Beneficiary which paralleled the concept of Core Customer common in the for profit world. None of them had ever considered that Kenaston might narrow its focus to a particular kind of person. Weren't they mandated to accept anyone who walked through their doors? The notion was met with a skeptical hesitancy. Tim encouraged them to engage the process with an open mind which they agreed to do.

As Tim led them through the exercise, he invited them to think of a resident who had made significant progress through her involvement with Kenaston. The group quickly identified Joanne as a person who fit that description. Tim asked them to see Joanne not just as a resident but as a real person, just like them with her own set of needs, fears, desires, hopes, and dreams. He then asked them to identify what needs, fears, desires, hopes, and dreams Joanne had as she entered Kenaston. They quickly identified Joanne as a women with mental health challenges who needed a supportive community where she could develop healthier coping mechanisms. She was willing to admit that she had a problem but more than that she was open to receive help and was motivated to engage the process to make the required changes. Given her background she was a woman who could benefit from some training in basic life skills. She desperately wanted to break out of the cycle of chronic homelessness which had been her experience but needed a hand up, not just a hand out.

Tim affirmed their work gaining clarity related to their core beneficiary. Pushing them further, he asked them how their current screening process helped identify the Joanne's who came through their doors. They acknowledged that the current screening process did little to help identify those who were most willing to recognize their need for help and motivated to make the necessary changes.

Brand Promise

Having made significant progress on identifying their Core Values, Core Purpose, BHAG, and Core Beneficiary Tim introduced the next exercise which caused most of them to do a double take! "Let's talk about your brand promise. What can you promise your residents, donors, partner agencies and volunteers that you're confident you will deliver with a high degree of excellence and consistency?"

Brand promise? That was something that fit for profit businesses but none of them had ever thought of it related to the world of nonprofits. Tim's question had revealed another important gap. "This exercise will build on the work you've already done. Your brand promise should reflect your core values, your core purpose, your BHAG and should fit with your Core Beneficiary." As they worked in their table groups an overarching brand promise emerged with three qualifying promises. The group agreed that the overall brand promise was going to be "Real Help for Real People." That was rooted in the commitment to address the underlying causes of episodic and chronic homelessness not just the symptoms and do that in a way that recognized each resident was real person with a story not just a statistic within the larger system. The three brand promises they wanted to make sure they delivered on with a high degree of excellence and consistency were, We will treat you with respect and dignity, provide compassionate care, we're focused on your long-term mental health.

Tim was pleased with their work and assured them that if they became intentional about measuring their effectiveness in delivering on these brand promises, their residents would be the beneficiaries of the improved focus, and their donors and funding partners would have greater assurance that their funds were being put to good use. Despite that affirmation of their group work, he pressed on and engaged them in another exercise that would add more rigour and focus to the day to day operations.

Actions to Live By

The exercise was introduced with the question, "Having identified your Core Values, Core Purpose, BHAG and Brand Promise, what are the actions you need to consistently live out in order to keep these aspects alive in your organization?" As they contemplated the question, they were quickly getting the sense that this process was not just about dreaming at a macro level, this process was also focused on the micro level with built in accountabilities to ensure the planning process moved from thinking and talking, to tangible, consistent implementation, measurement, and monitoring!

Their discussions focused most specifically on implementing accountability structures and metrics, both of which were noticeably lacking. The action they agreed was most critical was regular communication between management and front line workers related to the Core Values, Core Purpose, Brand Promise, and BHAG. The current communication was haphazard at best. The first identified action was regular, clear, and consistent communication and dialogue. Recognizing that their weekly Management Team Meeting agenda was usually driven by a crisis, they agreed that these meetings needed to be driven by their strategic priorities which was the second identified action. The third identified action was implementing regular performance reviews at every level of the organization. These performance reviews should focus on individual job performance as well as living out the core values. Those were unanimous that those performance reviews should be conducted with the management team first! The fourth action they agreed to was weekly meetings with the various departments within Kenaston. This would dramatically improve the communication and alignment throughout the organization. The fifth action which Donna presented as a non-negotiable were weekly meetings between Donna and individual members of the Executive Management Team. This would provide for focused conversation and strategizing with each management team member. Intuitively they all knew these actions would dramatically increase the accountability and alignment within Kenaston. They also knew that a significant culture shift was already taking place and not everyone would be open to the changes. Even those who were open to the changes would not find the process easy. Deep down they knew that without this kind of intentional and strategic shift, Kenaston was in trouble moving forward.

Chapter 13
Strategic Thinking/Execution Planning

The notion of strategic planning is enough to generate a glazed look in the eyes of even the most dedicated and motivated leader. I suspect you're no different. It's not a process you'd willingly choose to be involved in and for good reason. I met with the Executive Management Team of a potential nonprofit client and outlined for them what a planning process would look like should they agree to contract my services. As I invited questions after my presentation, I was shocked by the first question, "So are you telling us that we won't talk about where the plants should go in the lobby and who should be responsible for taking care of them?" Taking a moment to mask my shock, I responded, "There must be a story there!" I was then informed that they had an internal "expert" within their broader network facilitate a strategic planning process and the major outcome of that process was the location of the plants in the lobby. What I found profoundly saddening was that they weren't joking! They were completely serious. I assured them that if that was the most important priority they identified coming out of a process facilitated by me we'd have a serious "Come to Jesus" conversation. I could tell they wanted to believe me but were understandably skeptical given their previous experience. They did agree to engage my services and we set a date to begin the strategic thinking process.

As I work with nonprofit and social sector organizations there are several consistent patterns I encounter. First, the extent of the planning process in most of these organizations is to repeat what they've done the year before. The real "visionary" organizations tweak what they've done in the past. There's one small problem with that. Okay, it's a BIG problem. What worked yesterday worked in the world of yesterday. The world of today is different than the world of yesterday and the world of tomorrow will be exponentially different than the world of yesterday and today! What's required is not tweaking but entrepreneurial thinking on the part of the Executive Management Team and the Board of Directors! The nonprofit organizations who are going to not only survive but thrive will be required to think outside the box! That won't require them to abandon everything that's worked in the past but it will require a willingness to face the brutal facts, consider the dominant trends that are shaping the way in which fundraising, program development, service delivery and clients needs are impacting current and future reality. Government funding is not as plentiful as it once was and many of the grants available through the traditional funding sources have been dramatically reduced. Donors are more discriminating in selecting their charity of choice. They have higher expectations related to reporting and accountability and will be more amenable to support those organizations that not only measure expenses but also have identified program outcomes which are measured on a consistent and credible basis.

The second pattern I encounter is that even if an organization has a formal, structured planning process, the implementation of that plan usually doesn't happen with any degree of rigour, accountability and consistency. It matters little that the Executive Management Team and the Board of Directors had an off-site kumbaya experience if that experience doesn't in some way exert a tangible and dramatic impact on the day to day operations of the organizations moving forward.

If there is a formal process, there's no great clarity across the organization related to Core Values, Core Purpose, Core Beneficiary or BHAG. Core values are more often aspirational and they're rarely reinforced or measured. Core purpose is assumed but rarely clarified. The organization is committed to "being all things to all people" and hampered in its effectiveness because of its lack of focus. If there is a BHAG, it's vague and abstract with no tangible metrics to help measure progress towards that envisioned grand future.

In that sense it's far more helpful to abandon the notion of a strategic planning process in order to embrace a strategic thinking process. The typical strategic planning process is focused on discovering the right answers rather than embarking on journey to discover the right questions. As Tim helped Kenaston reframe their understanding of the process, they focused on the right questions which yielded a much more significant, albeit painful outcome. What's even more helpful is developing a strategic thinking culture where strategic thinking is not just an annual event, but an everyday occurrence. Imagine what might happen in your organization if most important management conversations were shaped by an underlying commitment to thinking strategically with a focus on asking the right questions?

Developing a strategic thinking culture is one of the primary responsibilities of the Executive Director and the Board of Directors. Good governance demands nothing less! This requires a particular skill set and discipline. If it's not modelled and reinforced by the key point leader and the Board, others in the organization will never embrace it as the "new normal." A strategic thinking culture is one where Core Values are celebrated, reinforced, and shape everything the organization does. The Core Purpose is the dominant mantra that is regularly repeated throughout the organization. There is focused attention to screening, identifying and responding to those who fit the Core Beneficiary description, and a corresponding willingness to say no to those who don't. That's hard for most nonprofits because they feel as if they're in some way being harsh, insensitive and cruel, but this clarity of focus allows them to maximize their impact for the people they are best suited to serve! A strategic thinking culture is driven by some overarching questions as they consider new program and service delivery opportunities. "Does it fit with our core purpose?" "Will it help meet the needs of our Core Beneficiary?" "Will it help us make significant progress in realizing our BHAG?" "Do we have the resources in place to meet this opportunity without jeopardizing our existing programs and services?" If the answer to each of those questions is a resounding "yes" the opportunity should be pursued and a plan developed for implementation and monitoring.

Execution Planning

Developing a strategic thinking culture is an important first step but it must move to the point of execution planning. This is where the vision begins to become reality and impact the day to day operations and organizational management plan. Having identified and articulated the foundational components, components which won't change a lot moving forward, what are the logical next steps to help see the BHAG move from the dream stage to reality?

3-5 Year Targets

The first step is to identify 3-5 year targets for the organization and that process is initiated by focusing on some strategic questions. Where do we want to be in 3-5 years in terms of funding, expenses, net income, partnerships, and reserves? Most of these categories will not come as a surprise with the exception of perhaps net income and reserves. Most nonprofits don't tend to focus as much on net income or accumulating cash reserves as they need to because they operate on a day to day, month to month basis related to cash flow. Part of that is due to the fact that their management plan tends to be much more reactive than proactive, responding to crises rather than thinking entrepreneurially. A strategic thinking culture fosters entrepreneurial thinking and helps expedite the shift from a reactive management paradigm to a proactive one.

3-5 Year Key Thrusts/Capabilities

With the 3-5 year targets identified, the next step is to identify the 3-5 year key thrusts and capabilities. Identifying these is shaped by addressing the following questions. If these are our core values, if this is our core purpose, and if this is our BHAG, what are the 3-5 key thrusts and capabilities we need to focus in on as an organization to live out our core values, better serve our core beneficiary, address current identified challenges and gaps, and help us make meaningful, focused progress towards our BHAG?

Getting clarity on the most important priorities is sometimes a difficult process. Typically the executive leadership team will be driven by the tyranny of the urgent and feel a compulsion to identify more than 3-5 priorities. What works best is to focus on the 3-5 highest priority items and invest energy gaining significant traction on those few priorities rather than marginal progress on a broader list of priorities. This requires the courage to say no to the good in order to say yes to the best! Expect that it will involve debate and disagreement but that's not necessarily a bad thing. It will require facing the brutal facts, accepting reality as it is without sugar coating it, and then committing to pay the price to move forward in an intentional and more focused way to make the biggest impact on the critical priorities.

3-5 Year Outcome Indicators

Equally important as identifying these key thrusts and capabilities is to quantify the desired outcomes and the outcome indicators. This addresses the question, "How will we know if we're making progress and what kind of progress we're making? Not just progress but the right progress towards seeing our BHAG realized? This drives the conversation to identify specific, measurable, and tangible outcomes, something many nonprofits struggle with. In response, and to their detriment, they avoid the struggle oftentimes hiding behind what appears to be noble reasons but in essence they're little more than excuses. Getting clarity on the specific outcomes that will help the organization as a whole tangibly measure its progress in achieving the 3-5 year key thrusts and capabilities energizes the entire organization because no one is left to guess as to what constitutes a "win". The goal posts are clearly marked and we know where they are! Everyone knows they're playing on the same team and heading to same end of the field so to speak.

1 Year Goals and Initiatives

With the 3-5 year targets identified, the focus shifts to the upcoming 12 months. Given the identified 3-5 year targets what are our goals for the next year? Where do we want to be 12 months from now related to funding, expenses, net income, partnerships, and reserves? This bring the longer term vision and strategy much closer to the immediate context.

In addition to the 1 year goals, it is important to identify the 3-5 key initiatives to be addressed and implemented in the next year. These emanate from the 3-5 year key thrusts and capabilities. "Given our identified 3-5 year key thrusts and capabilities, what initiative do we need to engage in the next 12 months to make progress towards those 3-5 year priorities?"

In my work with nonprofits what I have observed as teams

engage this process is team alignment becomes much more focused along with a growing consensus as to the kinds of initiatives which ought to occupy the organization's focus and energy in the upcoming year. Even though the process sometimes involves intense debate and disagreement, in a strange way there is a positive energy that builds as the team recognizes the benefits of having the difficult conversations, facing the brutal facts and developing a shared sense of direction guided by clearly outlined priorities.

The execution planning process is as important as the strategic thinking process in that it closes a loop that is often left gaping wide in most nonprofits. This is where the strategic thinking transitions from the realm of theory to practise and implementation. This is where the theory begins to exert a profound influence on the day to day operations in a way that dramatically increases the likelihood that significant progress will be made towards seeing the BHAG realized. This is where good intentions and passion are translated into focused action that exponentially increases the nonprofits opportunity to maximize its impact for its core beneficiaries, yielding the greatest return on investment of donor and partner agency funds. This is also where the executive leadership team realizes in a fresh and challenging way the price to be paid if the organization is to not only survive but thrive. In many ways it is a defining moment in the life of the organization. This is where the rubber hits the road. This is where passion is turned into proactive motion. This is the organizational pivot point. Those who choose to pay the price move forward in a synergistic and energized fashion. Those who don't are doomed to status quo, oblivious to the dire consequences of their choices or the destination they're headed toward.

Quarterly Rocks

You might be tempted to think that the execution planning process is done but it's not! Identifying quarterly "rocks" or priorities brings the strategic thinking and execution planning process into the immediate present. 3-5 year key thrusts and initiatives can be overwhelming as can 1 year initiatives. Identifying quarterly rocks makes the implementation plan much more manageable and attainable. Identifying these rocks involves reviewing the annual goals and initiatives and outlining specific actions that need to be undertaken in the upcoming 90 days along with a specific timeline for each item and one person tasked with the responsibility for each of the quarterly rocks. Resist the urge to have more than one person responsible for each of the rocks. If more than one person is responsible for a rock, no one is responsible. If the task doesn't get completed who do you hold accountable?

Individual Quarterly Priorities

The execution planning process is most effective when the process goes one step further to have each member of the Executive Management Team outline their own quarterly priorities. These priorities must be shaped by and aligned with the quarterly, annual, and 3-5 year priorities. Rarely does a conventional strategic planning process permeate the organizational structure to this level. That contributes to the failure of many strategic plans when it comes to implementation. Drilling down to this level exponentially increases the likelihood of implementation.

Having each Executive Management Team member identify quarterly priorities and share those with the rest of the team begins to build accountability within the team. There are no secrets. Team members have opportunity to provide feedback on the individual quarterly priorities of other team members.

They know what each team member is focused on and everyone has a very clear sense of how and where they contribute to the organization's progress towards its BHAG. The organizational impact is significant. No longer is work about just going through the motions or drudgery. To the contrary. Work comes alive. There is a sense that work has purpose. Executive Management Team members begin to see much more clearly how their work serves to make a tangible difference in the life of the organization and the lives of the core beneficiaries. As they capture that new sense of purpose, it reverberates throughout the organization to front-line workers.

Remember that potential client I referenced earlier in the chapter. After we had completed our initial strategic thinking/execution planning process, the business manager came to me and with tears in her eyes said, "Thank you. You've changed my perspective on strategic planning!" The Executive Management Team of that nonprofit embraced the process with passion, discipline, and rigour, and the impact on the organization has been nothing short of transformational. A member of a broader network of social sector agencies they are required to undergo an accreditation process every three years. Their previous accreditation process had not gone well. They failed to reach the required minimum of 80% in each of the five categories: Governance & Management; Human Resources; Facility; Spiritual & Religious Care; and, Community & Family Services. One of the required action items coming out of the accreditation report was to engage a formal strategic planning process which led them to contact me. Three years after engaging my coaching services and consistently implementing the strategic thinking/execution planning process, they went through the accreditation process again. With their scores in the previous accreditation report in the mid 70's, there was some anxiety as to what this report would reveal. When the results were released, they were informed they had and average score of 96% in each of the 5 categories! You can only imagine the sense of satisfaction, accomplishment, and excitement shared by every member of the Executive Management Team Member and staff! Deep down they knew that they were a completely different organization than they had been three years earlier, but it was good to receive that affirmation and recognition from those outside the organization who had conducted the accreditation process.

Chapter 14
Kenaston House - Execution Planning

As David reflected on the progress made so far, he was glad he had pushed the Board to contract Tim to facilitate and lead the process. While the process had just begun, David felt much more comfortable that he did in fact have a growing sense of what was going on with Kenaston House. He recognized that his level of liability as a Board member had decreased dramatically because of what they'd accomplished already. In a sobering kind of way he wondered why it had taken a crisis for the process to begin. He wasn't going to dwell on that, he was going to allow himself to fully engage Tim's process for the good of Kenaston.

Tim wouldn't allow the group to get comfortable or relax. Having accomplished some significant work and laid a much more solid foundation, he pressed on in a way that gently but firmly invited the entire team to move with him, which they did without resistance. It was like they had been waiting for a process like this to unfold without even realizing it.

Tim introduced the concept of execution planning as the natural next step to ensure they continued to build on the strong work they had accomplished so far. While none of them had heard it expressed quite the way Tim explained it, it made sense to them. They got it! At the same time they realized it was something that had been seriously lacking at Kenaston. They had no identified program outcomes. They had no clearly articulated goals with corresponding metrics. Nobody knew how to define a "win" or what constituted a "win." There was a sense of anticipation as they followed Tim's lead in the execution planning component of the process.

Tim circulated post-it note pads and asked each person to

take five post-it note. Puzzled they did as instructed. Once everyone had their allowed five post-it notes, Tim asked each of them to identify what they saw as the top five priorities Kenaston needed to focus on in the next 3-5 years and gave them fifteen minutes to complete the task. As he circulated the room, he noted that there were some common themes emerging within the group. At fifteen minutes he called the group back together and asked them to take their five priorities and posted them on a wall in the room. He then selected one Executive Management Team member and one Board member to group the individual priorities in themes. He knew what the outcome would be but they didn't. As the two began reviewing the identified priorities they were surprised at the synergy evidenced in the post-it notes. When they had completed the task, Tim called the group together and moved over to the wall and asked the Executive Management Team member to talk about how they had grouped the priorities and the categories represented in the identified priorities. As the rest of the group listened they were shocked at the alignment and synergy reflected in the responses. Without having talked about it as a group they were tracking in the same direction!

Reflecting on the identified priorities, intentional program planning, measurable outcomes, developing structured case management plans, improving the staff hiring process, and implementing more structured and regular performance reviews were clearly the most pressing priorities requiring their attention as an Executive Management Team. As Tim polled the group there was unanimous agreement that a focused effort to address these key areas would dramatically increase Kenaston's ability to make significant progress on the most important challenges facing them as an organization and they would make meaningful progress towards realizing their BHAG.

Tim pressed them further and challenged them to consider the financial implications of their BHAG and the priorities. Addressing these priorities and making meaningful progress toward their BHAG would require increase financial resources. This was music to Jennifer's ears! This was her opportunity to have significant input. Tim introduced a tool to help guide and focus their conversation. He called it the "Power of One" tool. "What if you could increase your revenue by 1%? What if you could decrease your program and operational costs by 1%? What it you increased your funding and donor base by 1%? What if you could increase your accounts payable by 1 day? What if you could decrease your accounts receivable by 1 day? I know that 1% doesn't sound like a lot but play along with me on this exercise. What impact would 1% or 1 day in these key areas have on your net income?" The wheels were turning for Jennifer because she knew the impact would be significant! She was convinced that none of her Executive Management Team colleagues or the Board fully understood how big of an impact that would have on their net income! As she began to provide some of the financial numbers for each of the categories Tim had identified they began the process of calculating the 1% for each category. The shock that began to ripple through the room was noticeable. 1% really could make a significant difference! By they time they had completed the exercise everyone realized they had more than recouped the costs associated with contracting Tim and generated a significant amount of additional money that could be channelled to program development and staffing. Beyond that they could begin to build a reserve fund that would become seed money for the additional building they would require if they were going to realize their BHAG! It wouldn't provide all the money they needed but it would give them a base upon which to build. They would need to engage a capital fundraising campaign but at this point in time there were more important priorities demanding their attention. They would need to keep the fundraising campaign on their radar to ensure that it didn't get lost in all of the other important activities and priorities that had been developed.

Having identified the 3-5 year priorities, Tim challenged them to focus on the next 12 months. "What do you need to focus your energies and attention on over the next 12 months,? What specifically will you do? Who will be responsible for each action? When will that action be completed? How will you measure progress?" What became crystal clear to everyone was that this was a process where it was going to be more difficult to hide or fudge the numbers if they followed through on what they were working on!

As they collaborated on articulating annual priorities, they agreed that communicating the outcomes of the strategic thinking/execution planning process to all of the staff was critically important. There was unanimous agreement that the communication plan was a vital component of the culture shift that was unfolding. If that culture shift was going to take root, everyone in the organization would need to know what the new "normal" was going to be. Donna was tasked to make sure the communication plan was implemented with a timeline of 9 months assigned to the initial phase of the process.

The second priority they identified was the need to implement a more consistent performance review process. Donna was tasked to develop the format in consultation with the Executive Management Team and implement it within 6 months. Donna would conduct the performance reviews for the management team and each manager would be responsible to conduct the performance reviews for their direct reports.

The third priority they identified was the need to review

every aspect of Kenaston's operations to determine the degree to which the Core Values, Core Purpose, and Brand Promise were active and alive in the organization. Each manager was tasked with initiating the review in their department and report back to the team within 90 days.

A fourth priority identified the need to review the core programs and services with a view to determining alignment with the foundational elements developed in the process facilitated by Tim. Brad was tasked to conduct this review in concert with Donna with the goal to have the thorough review completed by the end of the 12 month timeframe.

The fifth priority focused on people. They acknowledged there was a need to review every staff person with a view to evaluating their competence to do their assigned task, their compliance with the core values, and their long term fit with Kenaston. They agreed that this should be approached from a coaching perspective, providing every employee the opportunity to thrive in their role with the appropriate coaching. Where there was an unwillingness or an inability on the part of an individual to live into the new reality, the employee should be transitioned out and a replacement hired who fit with Kenaston's he core values and core purpose and also possessed the required skills to perform the tasks associate with the role. Donna agreed to coordinate this process in collaboration with the Executive Management Team.

They also agreed that this same process should be undertaken with volunteers as well. Some of them were not completely comfortable with this and verbalized this. How could you hold volunteers accountable to live out the core values, core purpose, and expect them to have a required skill set to serve the organization? Tim gently reminded them that each volunteer constituted a human face of the organization. they represented Kenaston and if they didn't reflect the core values, core purpose and execute their responsibilities with a high degree of excellence, that would reflect negatively on Kenaston. Jeff Miller chimed in with his support indicating that he had employed a similar process in his previous role and done so with great success. He indicated that most volunteers welcomed the increased emphasis on excellence and alignment with very few transitioning out. What had been even more surprising was the calibre of people stepping up to volunteer increased dramatically!

As they reflected on the annual priorities, there was agreement that focused attention on these priorities would help them address the issues most hampering and limiting Kenaston's ability to maximize its impact. There was a clear sense that if they could make significant progress on even half of these priorities they would be much further ahead than they were now. They were committed to make progress on all of the annual priorities, not just half!

Having identified the annual priorities, Tim led them through a process of identifying the specific activities and actions they wanted to engage in over the next 90 days coming out of the annual priorities. The group found this exercise incredibly helpful in providing smaller, tangible, and focused steps to help increase the implementation of the execution plan coming out of the strategic thinking. For each of the annual priorities they were able to identify tasks with clear, measurable outcomes to be completed within the next quarter. Everything was recorded so that there was no ambiguity as to the task, the person assigned to the task, or the timeline for completion.

For the sake of time, Tim circulated individual quarterly priority worksheets to each member of the Executive Management Team and to David as chair of the Board. They agreed that all members of the Executive Management Team would have their individual quarterly priorities completed by the next weekly management team meeting and report back to the team at that meeting. David agreed that the Board would complete their quarterly priorities at their regular scheduled Board meeting which was taking place the following week.

Tim then made a definite shift in his engagement with the group. There was seriousness that emanated from him. Turning to Donna he said, "Donna, it's your job to ensure that this strategic thinking and execution planning process gets implemented in every aspect of the organization. This process has involved your Executive Management Team but you have to ensure that this filters down to permeate every aspect and every department of Kenaston." He was very intentional in outlining this. He wanted to make sure everyone knew who was ultimately responsible for rolling this out ensuring that it impacted the day to day management of Kenaston. Donna loved what she was hearing! That was her understanding of her role as Executive Director and she was glad that Tim had reinforced that with the group as a whole.

Tim then shifted his focus to David and the Board. "David, it's your responsibility as chair of the Board to ensure the Board has clear processes in place to hold Donna accountable to execute on the plan and the priorities that have been developed and identified as a result of this process. There needs to be a disciplined focus on the part of the Board to ensure this plan is implemented with clear, concise, and regular reporting related to metrics and outcomes. Your Board meeting agendas must be driven by the strategic priorities and you must continue to engage strategic thinking at your Board meetings and Executive Management Team meetings. Strategic thinking must become a part of the organizational DNA not just a 2 day off-site activity. You could have done some things differently in your past, but you can't change your past. You can change your future and that starts today. It's really up to you as a group in terms of how this rolls out. If you do nothing with what we've accomplished, then you've wasted your precious time, your donors hard-earned contributions, and you've failed your core beneficiaries. I know that's not your heart but be prepared that this is going to take hard work, but it's a process worth investing every bit of your best time and energy into!"

While David and the Board felt somewhat chastised by Tim, they didn't feel belittled or shamed. They knew he was in their corner and he was helping them face the brutal facts because he genuinely cared about them as a Board and an Executive Management Team and he believed in the important work they were engaged in. Deep down they knew they were responsible for the governance oversight of Kenaston and they needed to be more diligent and disciplined in carrying out their legal and moral duty as a Board.

When Tim had finished, Donna asked Tim if she could speak. Addressing the group she informed the Executive Management Team that she was going to initiate daily huddles - short 10 minute meetings where they would connect to share a win from yesterday, identify what they were focused on today, and an area where they were stuck or needed help. This would continue to build the sense of alignment and accountability within the team. There was a collective sense of affirmation that rippled through the group. The Executive Management Team knew this would improve their level of implementation of the plan and the Board had an increased sense that they had made the right decision when they hired Donna as the new Executive Director. Even Brad was fully on Board with this plan. In a freeing kind of way, he saw that Donna possessed the skills and abilities he lacked. Kenaston was heading in a new, more focused direction that would enable it to dramatically improve its current program and service delivery and develop new strategic programs and services moving forward.

Chapter 15
Cash/Funding

People, strategy, and execution are three important areas every nonprofit needs to focus on. There is a fourth area that often dominates the most attention of nonprofit executive leaders and boards at the expense of these three, and that is the subject of money. Rarely do nonprofits have an abundance of disposable cash let alone cash reserves. Cash flow management consumes a lot of energy constituting a delicate juggling act between available cash and demands for the allocation of that cash. Perhaps this is where solid business practises and principles are most often compromised or ignored outright. Thriving nonprofits have realized the perils of ignoring solid business principles and have opted instead to implement those principles recognizing they owe it to their donors, funding partners, and beneficiaries to be responsible with every dollar that is donated to the organization and every dollar that is spent in carrying out its programs and services.

Gaining strategic alignment and clarity is critical when it comes to the aspect of cash flow management and funding. Evaluating every program and service using the following criteria is helpful in gaining this alignment and clarity.

First, what is the degree of alignment between the program and it's intended impact? Second, does it require funding or generate funding? A program that has a high degree of alignment with the intended impact and generates funding is a program that ought to be retained. The key is to invest in that program and grow it. If a program has a high degree of alignment with the intended impact but requires funding, the challenge is to pursue funding sources which will help fund the program on a go forward basis.

A program that has a low degree of alignment with the intended impact and requires funding or operates on a break-even basis is a program that needs to be re-evaluated. There are two options. If the program cannot be repurposed to increase the level of alignment and impact, serious consideration should be given to abandon ongoing involvement.

On the other hand, a program that has a low degree of alignment with the intended impact but generates revenue can quickly becomes a distraction to the organization. The temptation is to avoid the more difficult conversation because of the financial implications associated with abandoning the program. That being said, abandoning the program is not the only or even preferred alternative. It might be possible to adapt the program to increase its level of alignment and impact thereby retaining the revenue to the organization. The key point here is the ability to engage the difficult conversation driven by strategic thinking not just fiscal realities or pressures.

Having achieved a greater degree of strategic alignment and clarity related to cash and funding, a second exercise is equally relevant and important. Evaluating every aspect of the funding/donation/revenue cycle, program and service delivery cycle, operations cycle as well as the cash flow cycle with a view to identifying specific ways to improve each of those cycles is sometimes a painful but very profitable exercise. Painful in that it reveals inefficiencies present within the system which have been sapping valuable financial resources away from other areas which could have benefitted from adding financial resourcing. Profitable in that the organization is able to strategically allocate financial resources to those areas most deserving and worthy of the financial investment. This exercise requires an unprecedented level of ruthless candour to face the brutal facts and a corresponding courage to make the difficult decisions. It requires a courage to explore and implement best practises from like minded organizations and even businesses for the sake of increasing fiscal efficiency and responsibility. Often times doing what's right related to the new found efficiencies brings its own measure of pain. It may affect staffing levels, cutting programs or services a key stakeholder has a vested interest in. To make the tough choice might jeopardize funding or volunteer support. Sometimes this process requires abandoning processes that worked in the past but no longer work in the present. That disrupts the status quo which is rarely welcomed with open arms by those directly impacted by the change. As difficult and as painful as the decisions are, the long term sustainability and viability of the organization are in many ways dependent on courageous and decisive action.

A key reality which must be acknowledged and addressed that will dramatically impact the donor/funding cycle moving forward is the aging donor base of most nonprofit organizations. The donor base of most nonprofits is comprised of individuals who are baby boomers or older. Few nonprofits have engaged a strategic thinking process and developed a corresponding execution plan to broaden the donor base to include a younger demographic. The typical mechanisms used to connect with Baby Boomers and those older will not be effective in generating financial support from those within the demographic categories of Gen X, Gen Y, and Millennials.

While many nonprofit executive leaders and boards would prefer to bemoan their financial scarcity or crisis, few are prepared to engage the hard work of evaluating every aspect of the organization in the manner just outlined. That is not to minimize the reality of their situation but it is to place a higher degree of responsibility on the organization to think strategically related to their current financial reality and then develop plans that address current and emerging trends impacting donor and funding partner giving patterns.

Equally important in this conversation is the aversion to use the term "profit" within the context of nonprofit organizations. Call it net income, cash reserves or whatever moniker you want to attach to it, but if there is no net income, cash reserves, or profit, the organization is eventually doomed to financial ruin. It is both short-sighted and bad governance to consistently operate in that manner. Any business that consistently operates at a break-even or net loss is doomed to maintain the status quo, and will quite likely eventually be forced out of business. Why would well meaning people, deeply committed to doing good in the world through the nonprofit organization they're tasked to operate choose such a path of action? Don't the donors, funding partners, and beneficiaries deserve the same fiscal rigour and responsibility, employing proven business principles and practices in how the nonprofit manages the revenue generated and the monies expended in the delivery of programs and services? I would contend they do!

Chapter 16
Kenaston House - Fiscal Responsibility

Having introduced cash and funding into the strategic thinking conversation, Tim broached the subject of a more rigorous review of the business practises employed at Kenaston. You could sense the defensive apprehension of some within the group. The one person who was excitedly hanging on Tim's every word was Jennifer Moore. She knew there were efficiencies to be found within Kenaston which wouldn't in any way compromise the quality of program or service delivery. Previous attempts to initiate a similar conversation had always been met with strong resistance. "We're not a business!" was the common response. Jennifer knew that employing proven business tools and implementing business best practices in the day to day operations and budgeting processes within Kenaston could dramatically improve its ability to maximize its impact in the city! Sadly, she was a lone voice that was easy to ignore or silence. While she hadn't taken advantage of the opportunity to engage Donna in this conversation, she was apprehensive as to how Donna would respond. With Tim putting the issue on the table, she finally felt like she had an ally.

Having identified a significant "elephant in the room" the deafening silence from the group caught Tim's attention. "Why are you so quiet?" That only served to intensify the awkwardness in the room. Jeff, the newest member of the management team broke the silence. "What Tim is saying makes perfect sense to me! I think this is a conversation we need to have even if it's uncomfortable." Donna and Jennifer both agreed. Jennifer decided to throw down the gauntlet and spoke next. "I know there are ways that we can dramatically improve the efficiency of how we run things here at Kenaston and we can do that without in any way compromising the quality of our program and service delivery! In fact we'll actually be able to do what we do even better!" Tim was intrigued. "Why haven't some of those efficiencies already been implemented?" "That's been the one area where we have been stuck in a rut," Jennifer responded. As much as I appreciate and respect Nancy and the work she did in getting Kenaston established, she was not open to reviewing our operations and implementing the kinds of business practices and principles that I know could really benefit us!" Brad immediately chimed in, "To be brutally honest, I didn't have a clue about the finances so I know I wasn't much of a help to Jennifer." The level of transparency and authenticity was surprising. Nobody could remember this level of candour ever being expressed in a meeting at Kenaston. Board members who should have asked some of these kinds of questions had assumed that everything was in order but their eyes were now opened to a reality they were unaware of. They understood what Tim was saying because this is how they all operated in their for profit world. Tim reassured them they were not in any way abandoning their core values, core purpose or their BHAG by adopting proven business best practices and employing effective business tools. As an outsider to the system he could make those comments without any perceived agenda. Based on his experience with similar organizations he had seen the benefits this exercise had yielded for those organizations. While some were hesitant they all agreed that the conversation and ensuing process were critically important to Kenaston's viability and sustainability moving forward. So important that they agreed to add a thorough review of every aspect of their financial management to the previously identified 90 day priorities. Despite the fears and hesitation, this could not wait! It needed to be addressed sooner rather than later. Jennifer would be the one with ultimate responsibility but she would work hand in hand with Donna and the rest of the Executive Management Team in this review. It would be a collaborative effort and in a strange sort of way, there was cautious optimism that their fears were unfounded and the process might actually generate a positive outcome.

Tim assured them they had made significant progress as they engaged the process. They had greater clarity, focus and alignment as a group. They had identified some clear gaps but they had also put in place a plan to address those gaps in a proactive, strategic way. Transitioning to wrap up their session he asked them to provide a word or a phrase that summarized their sentiments reflecting on the time they had spent together. "Energized, empowered, excited, hopeful, focused, invigorated, cautiously optimistic, and renewed vision" were some of the responses. Tim reminded them that while they had made significant progress, the real work lay ahead as they moved to the implementation phase. Even those who had been resistant to engaging Tim's services left the session feeling good about what they had accomplished. While they entered the process skeptically resistant, they were all leaving as engaged participants, ready and willing to do whatever it took to move Kenaston forward. Before Tim let them disperse, they set a date for the first Quarterly follow up session with Tim. Tim reminded them that it was the ongoing discipline and accountability that would generate the greatest impact on the organization and ensure the most comprehensive implementation of the priorities they'd identified.

Chapter 17
Kenaston House - Implementation

Donna and David agreed to have lunch before the next Board meeting to debrief the process and strategize their plan of action moving forward. They both knew that a significant foundation had been laid but it was only the beginning. It would require persistent, proactive, decisive leadership on both their parts to ensure they maximized the benefit of the process that Tim had facilitated with them. Donna would be the key player in working with the Executive Management Team and David would be the key with the Board.

When they met for lunch several days later, they'd had time to debrief individually and their sentiments were no different several days removed from the process as they were when the process ended. They knew they had participated in something that would dramatically alter the way in which Kenaston functioned moving forward. It would dramatically alter the way the Board and Donna interacted, the kinds of things they would interact about, and it would significantly increase the level of accountability throughout the organization. All of those were good things. Neither of them were naive as to what it would require from then individually or from the Board and the Executive Management Team. They were both committed to pay the price, fully convinced that the return on investment for engaging Tim's services was going to be exponentially more than what they'd paid him.

They agreed on the key priorities that the Executive Management Team as well as the Board needed to devote their attention to. They talked about the composition of the Board and the Executive Management Team with a view to determining whether they had the right people in the right seats on the bus, focused on doing the right things right. There was no doubt that the Executive Management Team was stronger than it had ever been! This was a sign of significant progress. While there were questions related to some of the Board members, they both agreed that there was no urgency to re-place any of the current Board members. They would observe how some of the more reluctant Board members responded to the unfolding process moving forward before making any changes.

As Donna met with the Executive Management Team for the first time following their sessions with Tim, there was an uncharacteristic vibrancy and energy within the team! They were motivated, on board, and they wanted to get to work on the priorities they had identified in the session with Tim. As they took some time to debrief their individual experience of the session, it was clear that each management team member had taken time to reflect further on some of the conversations that had taken place with Tim. Donna was encouraged by that. Jeff, the newest member of the team posed a rather prob-ing question. "If dignity is one of our core values, does the way we run our programs reflect that?" "What are you think-ing?" Brad asked. "Well, does housing women in a dormitory like shelter facility with 30 other women reflect what it looks like to treat them with dignity? We serve those women meals in the cafeteria on paper plates, they drink out of styrofoam cups, and they use plastic utensils." Is that what dignity looks like? There was a poignant silence as each of them realized they had some work to do! If dignity was one of their core values, it would require some dramatic changes in the way they delivered programs and services. They couldn't house women like inmates! They would have to alter their shelter arrangements. As they talked about the cafeteria setup they realized this would require an investment of cash to purchase real dishes, cutlery, glasses, and mugs. A core value of dignity demanded that! There was one voice of caution. "Real dishes will get broken!" Jennifer responded, "If one of our core values is dignity, then we have to be prepared to pay the price!" Donna was pleasantly surprised. This was going to be a relatively easy group to lead. They were starting to think strategically and they were asking the right, albeit tough questions.

Jennifer continued the conversation expressing her sense that there were some efficiencies they could realize that would more than cover the costs required to purchase the dishes for the cafeteria.

Brad too joined in the conversation suggesting that some of their existing programs needed to be modified to help bring greater alignment between the programs and the stated core values, core purpose, and BHAG.

Donna informed them that their first huddle would take place at 9 am the next day. She outlined her expectations of each team member for their first huddle. She wanted to make sure there was no ambiguity as to her expectations.

She also informed them that she would be in touch with each of them individually to set up their weekly meeting with her. She indicated that her agenda for the first meeting was to begin framing their individual quarterly priorities. She said she would expect them to have given some thought to their priorities in advance of the meeting and come prepared to discuss them in more detail and agree to a list of priorities.

What was very clear was the Kenaston House they had known, was no longer. This was a new day, a new way of doing things, new expectations, increased alignment, focus and energy! As much as things had changed and yet needed to change, there was a real excitement about the possibilities of the future. It would be a win-win for everybody, as long as they were willing to embrace the new order and get in step with it.

As Donna began implementing the daily huddles with the management team, the sense of alignment and accountability continued to strengthen. Team members began calling out their colleagues when they failed to deliver on what they had indicated were their priorities. They were equally willing to offer support to team members who were stuck. The sense of camaraderie and trust grew rapidly as they realized they had each other's backs and were committed to the success of the team as a whole, not just their own.

Donna went to work developing the communication strategy. This was going to be a critical component of the implementation plan. The communication would need to clear, concise and consistent and whatever the message was, it would need to be modelled and lived out by Donna and the rest of the Executive Management Team. That would be the most powerful impetus for change with front line staff.

Having formulated a draft of the communication plan, Donna solicited input from the management team. They offered some minor tweaks to the plan which Donna willingly incorporated into the final document which only served to build trust between her and the rest of the team. She then scheduled a staff meeting for all full and part-time employees of Kenaston. Those who'd been around a while were shocked. This had never happened before! Donna outlined for them the process that Tim had led the Management Team and Board through, reviewed the Core Values, Core Purpose, BHAG, Brand Promise, Core Beneficiary, and Actions to Live By. She was clear to let them know that things were going to change at Kenaston and her hope was that every one of the staff would get on board with the changes and help take Kenaston to the next level in terms of its program and service delivery. She also informed them that compliance with the Core Values was non-negotiable and that applied to the Executive Management

Team just as much as it applied to each of them as staff. There would be formal more structured performance reviews that would be implemented and each department manager would meet with their direct reports for a weekly team meeting as a way of increasing team alignment, focus, and synergy within the various departments. There would also be a comprehensive review of every aspect of Kenaston's operation to ensure that the core values were being lived out across the organization, programs and services fit with the Core Values as well as the Core Purpose, and discover efficiencies that could generate more funding for new programs and services as those were identified by the Management Team.

There was one other point she emphasized with the staff. She wanted them to know that she was open to their input and feedback. She indicated that she knew they probably had ideas as to how Kenaston could increase efficiency and improve the quality of program and service delivery. She invited them to bring those suggestions up at their weekly team meetings assuring them that their manager would bring them up at the weekly management team meeting. What she said next stunned them. "If you see me violating one of our core values, you have the freedom to call me on it and hold me accountable to a higher standard! If I'm going to expect that of you, you have every right to expect that of me." Intuitively most of them knew that there was going to be no room for slackers! They were going to be expected to perform their job duties with excellence on a consistent basis. They also knew Donna shared that same commitment which only served to increase their respect for her as a leader.

During that first year following the initial consultation with Tim, Kenaston made significant progress. A year later it bore little resemblance to the Kenaston prior to Tim's strategic thinking/execution planning process. Weekly management team meeting agendas were driven by strategic priorities. Ironically the more they focused on strategic priorities, the less crisis they had to deal with. Most often they were thinking proactively and putting in place policies and procedures which circumvented most crises before they had a chance to gain momentum.

Unfortunately not all of the staff were as excited about the changes as Donna and the Executive Management Team. While they implemented much more of a coaching approach in their work with staff, some of the staff were clearly not a fit with the core values, core purpose or the requirements of their jobs. They were given every opportunity to modify their behaviour and that was always addressed in their performance reviews. Some were unwilling and others were unable to make the necessary adjustments and they were transitioned out, always with a generous and fair exit strategy. Some who had been lurking in the background prior to the changes emerged as shining stars! All they needed was the freedom and empowerment to thrive and offer more of who they were. They won, their team won, and Kenaston as a whole won. Once they got through some of the initial staff transition, improved their performance review and hiring process the level of staff transition decreased dramatically as did some of the "normal" drama which had characterized Kenaston for years!

Another significant change occurred in the relationship between Donna and the Board. Donna and David met on a regular basis. Donna was completely forthcoming with information related to the day to day operations of Kenaston as well as the progress on the implementation of the execution planning part of the process. The Board was much more engaged and asked the tough questions of Donna. They now understood that good governance demanded their complete and focused attention to issues of liability and risk, financial management, strategic direction, HR related concerns, Executive Management Team function, and performance reviews. The synergy and focus at Board meetings meant they were highly productive, fully able to debate and dialogue in a respectful manner with the primary focus being what was best for Kenaston House. As they moved through the year long engagement with Tim, their openness to change increased and their skepticism decreased. They could see the profound changes that were taking place and they had hope that the BHAG was not just a pipe dream. They were confident that they would see it realized!

Another key development over the course of that first year related to the evaluation of all of the programs and services that Kenaston engaged in. That review and evaluation was at times challenging and difficult. As the Executive Management Team engaged their respective departments in the review process, what became clear was that Kenaston was involved in programs and services that didn't fit with their core purpose and BHAG. This led to difficult conversations at the Executive Management Team meetings regarding whether Kenaston should consider abandoning some of the programs and services which they had been engaged with for a long time. As they continued to think strategically in asking the right questions, the Executive Management Team and the Board came to the conclusion that Kenaston could be more effective focusing their program and service delivery on fewer programs and services with an emphasis on quality and alignment not quantity and history. In a nutshell, they could do more by doing less and maximize the impact for their beneficiaries.

The other significant development that emerged over the course of that year had to do with their finances and cash flow. The operational review generated significant revenue that could be allocated for programs and services without compromising the quality of the program and service delivery. That was just as Jennifer had predicted.

Closely related to this was a focused intentionality in terms of Kenaston's communication with donors and funding partners. The Board and Donna committed to an increased level of transparency and authenticity in the communiques that were circulated to donors and funding partners. The response was surprising in that existing donors increased their financial support of Kenaston. Major funding partners became active advocates with other agencies encouraging them to direct funds to Kenaston given the significant transformation taking place. In addition, new donors began contacting Kenaston inquiring as to how they could begin supporting the work Kenaston was doing. Additional volunteers began to connect with Jeff Miller seeking opportunities to help out. These were very competent and skilled volunteers who embodied the core values of Kenaston and shared the same passion reflected in the Core Purpose.

As Tim continued to facilitate the strategic thinking/execution planning process, he looked forward to each opportunity to connect with the Kenaston team. They had become good friends and rarely had he seen a team of leaders engage a process so fully as the Kenaston team had. It gave him renewed faith that there actually were nonprofit organizations who were prepared to think entrepreneurially, step outside of the comfort zone, move beyond tweaking what they'd always done to learn new ways of doing things motivated by a profound belief that to do anything less was an abdication of their duty and commitment to do good in the world no matter what the cost! Kenaston became the "poster child" for nonprofits in the city, an example of what could be when you had a team of motivated, passionate, competent and skilled people, aligned and working together, focused on executing the highest priority activities with excellence on a consistent basis.

Chapter 18
Your Story

As I've indicated, the story of Kenaston House is a fable. There is no Kenaston House - at least not as far as I know. The scenarios reflected in the fable are true to life experiences coming out of real life nonprofit organizations. The power of fable is that it gives us permission to see ourselves, see our organizations in the ebb and flow of the fable. We can identify with the story and the characters. I'm hoping that as you've read that's been your experience. Not because I have some evil penchant to make you squirm in discomfort, but because I've worked with enough nonprofits over the span of my career to have seen these themes with profound regularity and consistency. I wish it wasn't so, but it is. I do know the stories of a minority of nonprofits who have been led by visionary, entrepreneurial, courageous leaders who have been willing to pay the same price Kenaston paid. I've seen what could be! I've seen the transformation that parallels the transformation at Kenaston House. That's what drives me. My core purpose is transforming communities one nonprofit at a time!

I'm going to make some assumptions about you. I know that's dangerous, but I'll risk it. Since you're reading this book, I'm going to assume that nonprofit organizations matter to you. Specifically nonprofits who think strategically, develop a plan based on that strategic thinking and then commit themselves to execute that plan with focused alignment, consistency, accountability, metrics, and excellence. I'm also going to assume that some are reading this book because you lead a nonprofit that's struggling with issues of viability, alignment, focus, and sustainability. You have good people who work in the organization but you probably don't have the best people working in every position within the organization.

Your pattern has most likely been to look back and tweak what worked in the past and you're coming to the realization that it no longer works. You're a good person who cares deeply about the cause you're invested in. You're driven by passion but hopefully by now you realize that passion by itself isn't enough. It could be that your organization is bound by some of the mythical core values I articulated in Chapter 4. Here's the good news. You are not a prisoner to your circumstances. You can break free of them but it will require courage, persistence, and fortitude.

I'm also going to assume that most who read this will not have clearly identified program outcomes with identified measurable outcomes that are monitored and measured on a consistent basis. I'm going to assume that you don't have clear accountability structures that continually call people to task completion encouraging them to rise to the next level in the execution of their job responsibilities, goals, and outcomes. I'm going to assume that in the nonprofit organization you lead or connect with, the Board of directors are passive observers to the strategic thinking/execution planning process rather than the catalysts driving the process.

I could be wrong on some of my assumptions, but I suspect that most of them are fairly true to life - for you. I've seen too many nonprofits that fit these assumptions and some nonprofits I've seen embody all of these assumptions! While I don't know your story, I do know many stories. You know your story better than I do.

Allow me to pose some questions for your consideration related to your story. What part or parts of Kenaston's story parallel your story? I guarantee there's at least one, probably more. Are you and the rest of your leadership team willing to take the hard look in the mirror, acknowledge your story for what it is - for better and for worse - embrace your story by facing the brutal facts leading to engaging an external resource to begin you own process of transformation similar to Kenaston? It's not about whether or not you have the expertise you need to initiate this process. It more about whether you have the courage to embrace the process. That's what it took for every member of the Kenaston management team and Board of Directors. It is primarily an act of courage, perhaps fuelled by a level of desperation that wakes you in the middle of the night in a cold sweat.

Here's another assumption I'm going to make. Some who read this will think to themselves, "We can do this ourselves. We don't need to spend the money to bring someone in to do it." That may be the case, but again, based on my experience, it rarely works as effectively as having an external facilitator lead the process. Think back to the story of Kenaston. Who do you think could have led that process internally with the degree of expertise, insight, and skill that Tim brought to the process? Having Tim facilitate the process, every one in the room engaged on a level playing field. Donna was a participant just like her direct reports. David was a participant just like all of the staff and the rest of the Board. There was no hierarchical pecking order - Tim was the one leading and facilitating the process. He had the expertise, skills, and tools which greatly enhanced the value of the process for Kenaston. He could ask the tough questions that an internal facilitator would have had much greater difficulty addressing.

A key question for you to wrestle with is this, "What is it already costing you in terms of lost productivity, misalignment, lack of focus, and no clear sense of direction?" That's a question most of don't want to face but it is costing you something. It's probably costing you a lot more than your realize. Sure it's hard to quantify but that doesn't mean you can't quantify it. The bigger question is, "Are you willing to do the hard work and face the brutal facts that emerge as the answer?"

If you simply tweak what you've always done where will your organization be at in 3-5 years? The key to long term viability for most nonprofits involves acknowledging that tweaking what worked in the past incorporates little by way of strategic thinking. Strategic thinking acknowledges that the world is changing and changing rapidly. It's challenging enough to keep up with the pace of change let alone get one step ahead. Like Kenaston, there are some nonprofits who have been able to make the shift. Will the organization you're a part of be one of those who keep pace with the changing world in which you operate or will you become a statistic or casualty of the change taking place around you?

If the organization you care about were to engage a process similar to Kenaston, what impact do you think it would have on your organization? On you? What changes would be required? What gaps might be exposed? What would be at stake for you personally as you consider engaging such a process? Whether you're a Board or staff member, there are associated risks and fears. Donna, David, and every other member of the management team and Board had no idea how the process would unfold, what surprises might emerge, or what the specific outcome would be. They were willing to walk into that uncertainty, manage their fear rather than allow their fear to manage them, and they reaped the benefits of that courageous step. Hopefully you found the outcome of their story inspiring. They are a part of the minority. In this case, being a part of the majority is not something to be championed or lauded.

As I've worked with nonprofits, I've seen a pervasive commitment to preserve the status quo as if there were no risks associated with the status quo. Sometimes the greatest risk, particularly in times of great change, is the fight to preserve the status quo. Sure, the status quo is predictable but sometimes holding to it is lethal.

Government funding for nonprofits is a dwindling and diminishing resource. Given the number of stories exposing nonprofit organizations who lack the rigour, discipline, transparency, accountability structures, measurable outcomes and best practises in term of their operational realities, donors and funding partners are much more discerning in choosing the charities who are worthy recipients of their charitable donations.

Most nonprofits champion the percentage of revenue that is allocated for administration. It seems that the credible benchmark of a "worthy" nonprofit is something less than 10%. Ironically few of those nonprofits provide any substantive data related to program outcomes. Does it really matter if your administrative expenses are less than 10 % of total revenue if your impact is negligible? Would it not be better for your administrative expenses to be 15-20% of total revenue which then enabled you to hire the best people for the job resulting in program outcomes 20X better as a result. That presumes you have identified program outcomes and a credible tracking mechanism. I'm not advocating for reckless spending related to administration but I am suggesting that it's important for nonprofits to measure administrative expenditures AND program outcomes. Dan Pallotta's fine work in this regard is worth implementing, however few nonprofits have the courage to follow through on that. What I find puzzling is that some large foundations require nonprofits to keep administrative expenses below 10% of gross revenue in order to be considered for and secure grant funding. Ironically some of these foundations are run by very competent, entrepreneurial business people who would never employ the same practise in their for profit businesses. Some would in fact deem it irresponsible to do so. Most reputable, successful business owners would focus first and foremost on hiring the best person for the job. Restricting nonprofits to administrative expenses of no more than 10% of gross revenue often makes that practise prohibitive for the nonprofit. Pardon the sarcasm but, "We spend less than 10% on administration but don't ask us what you get for that 10% because we can't tell you!" I know that sounds crass but in many nonprofits that's the brutal fact! Sorry for being an honest broker. If a funding partner agency had asked Kenaston to quantify their program outcomes, that's how they would been obligated to respond because they had no idea what their desired outcomes were nor did they measure any outcomes. They're not alone!

Take this concept and apply it to your nonprofit. What do you think the response would be? What would it be like for you to not only suggest it but actually implement it? If I were a betting person, I'd bet there'd be immediate and significant pushback from members of your Board, key donors and funding partners.

I have served on more than one nonprofit Board where accountability structures were non-existent. As the Board worked to put these these structures in place, the push back from staff was that the Board was too focused on business principles that weren't relevant in a nonprofit. Is that part of your story? If not, you're unique. If it is your story, would the response to implementing accountability structures be any different?

I know that each of these questions cut beneath the veneer of organizational life in your nonprofit but these are the components of your story that are important for you to understand, embrace, and reflect on.

Your organization has a story. What is that story? Not the

urban legend, the straight goods! What story is your cash flow telling you? Is it static, decreasing, increasing? What demographics are represented in your donor base? How many donors have begun supporting your cause within the last 12 months? Your cash flow is providing you a telling story but most nonprofits are illiterate when it comes to reading the story with any degree of accuracy.

I know it sounds like I'm being a bit harsh, but please understand that I believe in the cause you're invested in. I believe in the value of nonprofit organizations like yours. Enough so that I'm passionate about doing everything I can to help you write a new, more compelling chapter to your story. I'm committed to help you craft that chapter in such a powerful way that as you begin to tell that story there will be a flood of new support that lands on your door step because people want to be a part of the change you're committed to bring to your world! They will be caught up not only by your passion but by your plan!

Chapter 19
Entrepreneurial Leadership - The Way Forward

So what is the way forward? Is all hope lost? Not at all! Given the change taking place related to nonprofit funding, I'm prepared to defend rather vigorously the notion that only those nonprofits who are led by entrepreneurial leaders will be the nonprofits who will not only survive but thrive and grow. They're the ones who will be able to scale up their operations, increase their funding sources, maximize their impact and do the most good for their core beneficiaries and their communities.

What will that entail? Entrepreneurs are by nature risk takers. Good entrepreneurs are calculated risk takers. They have a dream and a plan. They see things before most other people do. They see things what others are blind to. Where others live in a world where, "That will never work!" Entrepreneurs live in the world of, "Oh yeah? Why not?" They stay awake at night figuring out why and how it can work! They're not afraid of success or failure and they're willing risk the latter to achieve the former. Some are reckless but not all. They ask the questions others are afraid to ask and the answers don't frighten or dissuade them from the journey they're on.

Entrepreneurs think outside of the box. Their default is not to look back, identify what worked in the past, and then tweak it. They're not disrespectful of the past but they recognize that the world of the past is different than the world of today and the world of tomorrow is exponentially different than the world of yesterday. They're aware of the past, they live in the present, and they look to the future.

For entrepreneurs, strategic thinking is integral to their DNA. They're on a search for the right questions more than the right answers. Once they discover the right questions, they are ruthless in their efforts to create answers that fit the future not the present or the past. Answers that address the identified deficiencies in the present and chart a course for a new, invigorated future. Entrepreneurs are often ruthless in their critique of what they perceive to be the flaws of the past and the present. They are driven by an idealism that envisions a future much different from the present and the past. They see further than others see.

Henry Ford is reported to have said, "If I had asked people what they wanted, they would have said 'faster horses.'" He envisioned a powered "horse" with four wheels instead of four legs powered by a combustible engine. Steve Jobs envisioned a hand held device capable of storing thousands of songs, effectively rendering the compact disc obsolete just as the compact disc had rendered the cassette and 8-track tape obsolete. This device would allow people to take their entire music collection with them listening to music "on the go." People scoffed at Ford and Jobs convinced they were doomed to fail. They were the laughing stock of many of their peers! Instead their fearfully cautious peers became the laughing stock! If you're reading this you are a beneficiary of entrepreneurial spirit of people like Henry Ford and Steve Jobs!

That raises an important and relevant question. At least it does for me. Who are the Henry Ford's and Steve Jobs' in the world of nonprofits? Who are the nonprofit leaders who are so innovative, courageous, and visionary that they're driven to create something other than a faster horse or a better compact disc for their nonprofit and others like them? Who are the nonprofit leaders who are so innovative they've become the laughing stock of their peers? There might be one or two, but my experience is that entrepreneurs don't choose to work in the nonprofit or social sector and if they do they don't survive for long. The pervasive commitment to maintain the status quo that exists within the world of nonprofits and the social sector either marginalizes their entrepreneurial impact or drives them out leaving them utterly frustrated and disheartened.

Execution planning is a second integral component of the entrepreneur's DNA. Good entrepreneurs engage the disciplined process of charting their course of action. Identifying the desired end goal, they begin to work back from that point, identifying each of the required steps in order to take them from where they are to where they want to be. Clearly defined outcomes, priorities, metrics, and accountabilities are built into their planning model. While this plan has form and structure, it has a fluidity to it as well. Entrepreneurs recognize that whatever knowledge they possess in the present, it continues to evolve as they progress towards their long term goal. Failure and setbacks along the way motivate them to press on, overcome the hurdles and obstacles, hone and refine their plan, drawn by the irresistible magnetic pull of the end goal. Criticism and critique are carefully filtered in an effort to discover the gold nuggets worth retaining.

Entrepreneurs have a bias for action. Having discovered and oftentimes created the answer to the right question, they move to prioritized action emanating from, and shaped by their clear, concise, and thorough planning process.

Entrepreneurial Implications for Nonprofits

What I'm proposing is an entrepreneurial approach to the way nonprofits think, plan, and manage their day to day operations. What will this look like for nonprofits willing to respond to the call and embrace the challenge? It will require a significant paradigm shift in the four key areas, People, Strategic Thinking, Execution Planning, and Cash/Funding.

People

The first, and perhaps most pronounced change will take place in the hiring processes. While passion is an important characteristic of every staff person, volunteer and Board member, entrepreneurial nonprofits will realize there are other more important characteristics which take precedence over passion but never at the expense of passion.

There will be a commitment to hire and retain people who consistently embody the organization's core values, share its core purpose, and possess an unusual ability and skill set to consistently execute the requirements of the job with a high degree of excellence and proficiency. This will require a dramatic and significant paradigm shift for most nonprofits. This is what successful businesses and entrepreneurs do and this is what successful nonprofits must do if they are to break with the past and aggressively engage the future. Their long term viability and sustainability depends on it! Without it they are doomed to tweak what's worked in the past, be bound by that past. This applies to paid staff, program volunteers, and Board members. It must permeate every aspect of the organization!

There are two "hires" that are critical to this paradigm shift taking root across the organization as a whole. The first hiring priority is the Executive Director or whatever title the key point leader holds in the organization. This person must fully embody the core values, and core purpose of the organization and have a proven track record of effective team leadership. This person must also be a strategic thinker, someone who can continue to prime the pump to help the organization focus on addressing the right questions. This person must have a strong business sense with a sensitivity to the realities that impact and shape the world of nonprofits. Employing best business practices in the organization must be championed by the Executive Director.

The second critical "hire" is the chair of the Board of Directors. While it's not a hire in the purest sense, the same processes employed in hiring paid staff need to impact the selection of this person. The chair of the Board must model to the rest of the Board and the staff as a whole the foundational values of the organization. If one of the key governance tasks of the Board is to hold the Executive Director accountable to the consistently live out the core values, core purpose, and make tangible, meaningful progress in achieving the 3-5 year, annual, and quarterly priorities, how can that occur with any kind of integrity if the Board Chair and the Board as a whole don't embrace and embody the very standards they're tasked to ensure are alive and well in the organization. The Board Chair must have a thorough and comprehensive understanding of Board governance with a proven track record of leading effective and successful boards. There should be no compromise in the process of securing the right people for these two critical positions within the organization.

A focus on getting the right person as the Executive Director and Board Chair will reap significant benefits for the organization as a whole. They will recognize the importance of clear, concise and relevant job descriptions accompanied by a rigorous and regular performance review process will be the norm not the exception. They will ensure the development and implementation of these critical components. No longer will "average" be good enough. Excellence will permeate and characterize every aspect of organizational life. Modelled and embraced by the executive leaders and Board of directors, employees and volunteers will embrace this paradigm, or they'll be redeployed to their next job with some other organization.

These employees will be compensated in a way that recognizes their value to the organization. That won't necessarily mean their compensation package will be on par with their for profit contemporaries, but no longer will they be expected to embrace subpar compensation for the sake of the cause! There will be an acknowledgement that a reasonable investment in people will yield positive results for the organization. This will require courageous leadership from the Board of Directors. Expect that there will be push back and resistance from some donors and funding partners. Not all, but some. These people must be compensated well for their work. No longer is the "we're just a nonprofit" mantra acceptable to justify substandard policies and practises in the hiring and compensation process!

Strategic Thinking

The second critical change will be a willingness to ensure the priority of strategic thinking as a critical component of the organization's DNA. No longer will tweaking what worked in the past be the predominant modus operandi. There will be a pervasive commitment to evaluate and mistrust the status quo recognizing that the organization carries out its mandate in a rapidly changing world. This will be characterized by a relentless pursuit of the right questions more than the right answers. The entrepreneurial nonprofit will be a place where the only question that is off base is the question that's not verbalized. No matter what your role in this kind of organization, you will now you have a voice and your questions are worth breaking the institutional silence!

With strategic thinking as a cultural norm, these organizations will make the investment of financial and people resources to engage in regular, structured, facilitated strategic thinking sessions involving the Executive Management Team and the Board of directors. The impact of engaging this process will be increased alignment, greater focus, productivity, and cohesion within the staff team and the organization as a whole. The return on investment will be exponential although realizing the full benefits will require patient persistence because culture change takes time.

Core values will be modelled, celebrated and reinforced. The organization's Core Purpose will be the dominant mantra staff and Board members recite in their sleep because it is so ingrained in their collective psyche! Every staff person and volunteer will have a clear and unmistakeable awareness of their part in the organization's mission, what constitutes a "win" and where the "goal posts" are located.

The BHAG will be the grid through which every decision, program initiative, modification or change is evaluated. The BHAG will shape the 3-5 year, annual, quarterly and individual priorities.

This process will involve an unbridled willingness to face the brutal facts, regularly review the organizational strengths and weaknesses and identify the significant trends which have the potential of impacting every aspect of the organization moving forward. The purpose of this review is to proactively evaluate current reality and prepare for what is coming down the road in advance of its arrival. This will serve as an antidote to the "tweak what we've always done" pattern of the past.

Execution Planning

Having achieved organizational "genetic modification" so

to speak by injecting strategic thinking into the cultural DNA, there will a invigorated bias for action putting clear, tangible, measurable goals and program outcomes in place, goals and program outcomes which are consistently monitored and measured which every department, employee, volunteer and Board member is held accountable to. This will be the norm not the exception. This will require courage, persistence and reinforcement. The status quo will balk, whine, and resist! Don't be surprised if you hear phrases like, "This will never work!   We're a nonprofit, not a business!" If you're leading the process, you'll be taunted and mocked just like the Henry Ford's, Bill Gates', Elon Musk's and Steve Jobs' of the world! Expect that some within your organization will be unwilling to embrace the way. A failure to address their unwillingness through coaching and decisive action will serve to undo some of the good work accomplished in the strategic thinking process. There must be no tolerance for noncompliance regardless of the person or position.

Management team members will regularly meet with direct reports, beneficiaries, donors and funding partners in an effort to gain important and relevant feedback as to how the organization is doing. While this feedback may be difficult and at times painful to receive, it is valuable feedback that can help the organization continue the strategic thinking process allowing the feedback to shape, inform and improve the quality of program and service delivery and overall organizational effectiveness. This data will also help determine the degree to which the organization is delivering on it's brand promise.

Meeting agendas will be driven by the goals and priorities not the tyranny of the urgent. Plans, goals, and outcomes will be reviewed on a regular basis to keep them relevant to current realities. Individuals who repeatedly fail to meet targets will be held accountable by team members. Planning sessions will be regular occurrences yielding updated goals, program outcomes and metrics. Team and individual victories will be celebrated, providing new and existing team members a tangible portrait of the behavioural and performance standards characteristic of the organization.

The net benefit of the increased discipline related to execution planning will be improved organizational alignment, focus, collaboration, employee/volunteer engagement, and job satisfaction, not to mention the increased inter-departmental sense of teamwork.

There is another by-product worth noting here. Entrepreneurial nonprofit leaders who commit to the process outlined thus far will be catalysts for organizational transformation. This will increase the organization's profile and credibility and will generate increase interest from competent, qualified individuals looking to join the team either as an employee or volunteer. It will also result in existing donors increasing their support of the mission and new donors and funding partners joining the mission.

Cash/Funding

The final key area to be impacted by entrepreneurial leadership is perhaps the area that consumes most of the Board and management team's energy and generates the greatest degree of stress is the matter of cash and funding.

The first major paradigm shift required as it relates to cash and funding is the acknowledgement that employing solid best business practises in the area of financial management and fiscal responsibility does not in any substantial way compromise the core values and core purpose of the organization. This is sometimes a painful and humbling admission for nonprofit executive leaders and Board members to make. Many have vigorously resisted this notion to their own detriment.

Unfortunately they have no idea how their stubborn defiance of sound financial management has created some of the very problems they have faced and wrestled with for quite a while. They are largely uninformed as to how a moderate dose of humility could dramatically reduce their stress level and improve the organization's fiscal foundation.

Investors Not Donors

One important shift that can serve to catalyze change is to view donors and funding partners as investors. While the change in nomenclature might seem to be a minor tweak, it actually represents a significant paradigm shift. Think about it from this perspective. If you own shares in a company, that company feels a sense of duty and responsibility to treat you with respect and dignity, keep you informed as to the company's performance and its impact on the value of your stock. The Executive Management Team and Board of Directors feel a duty to manage the day to day affairs in such a way to maximize the benefit to you as a shareholder. You receive notice of the company's Annual General Meeting and have an opportunity to have a say in the affairs of the company through your shareholder's vote.

What if nonprofit executive leadership teams and boards viewed donors and funding partners though the same lens? What impact might that have on the way in which they managed the day to day affairs, communicated with donors and funding partners and solicited their input in key decisions? I contend it would have a dramatic impact on the way in which they viewed the situation. If, for example as a shareholder of a company I learned that the Executive Management Team was vigorously resistant to employing best practises related to the financial management of the company, I would have serious and very valid concerns! Why shouldn't that be the case

144

with nonprofits as well? Why shouldn't donors and funding partners have the right to place the same expectations on those tasked with the executive leadership and governance oversight of the organization? Why wouldn't those same executive leaders wilfully offer full and transparent disclosure of all of the organization's affairs, financial and otherwise, to donors and funding partners? Why wouldn't they feel a responsibility to keep donors and funding partners informed on a regular and consistent basis? For many nonprofits this notion is viewed with skepticism and cynicism reflecting too much of a business perspective.

Moving forward, the nonprofit organizations that will continue to engender and earn trust with donors, funding partners, and the community at large will be those who treat donors and funding partners as investors - people and agencies making a financial investment in a cause that has clear, measurable outcomes, employing best practises in every aspect of the organization, hiring the best people for every position in the organization, recruiting the best volunteers and Board members so as to maximize the "shareholder's" return on investment. I know the terminology will rub some the wrong way but that doesn't negate the application or relevance for nonprofit organizations.

Profit is Not a Profanity

The second key shift related to Cash/Funding has to do with the term "profit." Many nonprofit organizations view it as a profanity, a word that should never be uttered in a conversation within or about the organization. REALLY? SERIOUSLY? Pardon my somewhat cynical shock.

What future does any nonprofit have if there isn't some "profit"? Call it cash reserves, net income or some other term you can live with. Living "hand to mouth" commonplace in most nonprofits is rarely deemed a responsible money management strategy. It matters little whether it's personal finances, government finances, business finances or nonprofit finances. No one would defend this as the best, let alone a good longterm financial management strategy. Surprisingly, this is the norm in many nonprofits. Perhaps it's time to embrace "profit" as a part of the fiscal vocabulary within the world of nonprofits. If your organization has a BHAG there must be financial implications connected with that BHAG. Few organizations have a Big Hairy Audacious Goal that doesn't require additional financial capital to see the BHAG realized. Entrepreneurial nonprofit leadership will embrace "profit" as a legitimate, responsible financial management strategy. The distinctive of this shift will be that the goal is never profit for profit's sake. The goal in accumulating profit is to facilitate the ongoing growth and development of the organization as well as ensure the longterm viability and sustainability of the organization and its mission.

Embracing the notion of "profit" will result in a more rigorous approach to the day to day management of the financial aspects of the organization. It will result in a organization wide commitment to identify operational efficiencies which could be realized without in any way compromising the quality and scope of program and service delivery.

The key thrust of the book Conscious Capitalism is that businesses need to move beyond profit for profit's sake and all the a socially responsible core purpose to drive the organization to make an impact beyond just profit. I would contend that while most nonprofits have a much clearer sense of their core purpose, they need to focus more on employing best business practises so that they can do even greater good in the world.

Employing the "Power of One" tool like Kenaston House

did would be another financial strategy that could reap significant cash flow management benefits to the organization.

Communicating more frequently and more transparently as to the financial situation with the organization is not only a good governance practise, it also serves to quickly build trust with investors! The more an organization is able to build that trust, those investors transition to become passionate evangelists for the cause - spreading the story to others they know. That constitutes the best unpaid advertising the organization has at it's disposal with a relative low input cost. In addition, it has the potential to yield significant positive financial "dividends" further enhancing the immediate cash position while improving the longterm viability and sustainability.

Nonprofits able to make this significant transition will soon make another significant transition. They will make the shift their gaze from the individual donors, who are each important and the backbone of the ongoing cash flow of the organization to focus on the larger donors. My experience is that many nonprofits are reluctant to talk money, especially when it comes to approaching donors who have the capacity to make a significant investment in the cause or larger foundations. They are cursed with a false sense of modesty, unaware of their credibility and uncomfortable to fully embrace and champion it when requesting new investor revenue.

So What? Now What?

Let's make another assumption. Let's assume that I'm 100% correct in every assertion I've made in the preceding pages. I'm not sure that's true but this is what I do know based on my first hand experience working for and with non-profits. I know that much of it is true - proven beyond a shadow of a doubt in the court of real life! So what? Now What?

If all you do is read this book and take no action as a result of what you've read, I'd be disappointed. I'm a catalyst for change. Remember my core purpose? Transforming communities, one nonprofit at a time. I'm not just about providing information, I'm about catalyzing transformation.

Let's talk about next steps. What are you going to do with what you now know? What are the areas you need to think strategically about? What's the execution plan you need to begin to put in place?

Whether you're a leader in a church, community-based nonprofit, faith-based nonprofit, or social sector agency, I know this works. I've facilitated this process with leaders in every kind of organization just mentioned. Each has its own unique dynamics but the fundamental principles apply and I know the tools work!

Here's some critical questions I believe can help you and your organization act in strategic and proactive ways as you reflect on the story of Kenaston House and your story and engage a process that will take you from where you are to where you could be.

• To what degree is strategic thinking a part of your organization's DNA?
• Do you have core values that are modelled by your Executive Management Team, and reinforced throughout your organization?

- Is your Core Purpose clear, understood, and embraced by everyone within your organization?
- What is your Big Hairy Audacious Goal? Is it measurable?
- Have you identified your Core Beneficiary? Do you have a concise description of what that person looks like and how you can meet their needs, wants, and desires?
- Do you have clearly identified 3-5 year, annual, quarterly, and individual priorities that are monitored and measured on a consistent basis?
- Do you have a hiring process that focuses first and foremost on getting the right people in the right seats executing the right things right with a high degree of consistency and excellence?
- What might change in your organization if you had a more structured, rigorous, and intentional hiring process?
- Do you have regular, structured performance reviews designed to help everyone within the organization grow and develop in the exercise of their job responsibilities in an effort to maximize the impact they make for the cause you're invested in?
- Do you have a clear strategy to broaden and develop your "investor" base to connect with a younger demographic?
- What are the significant trends already impacting or will impact the way in which you deliver programs/services, raise funds, recruit volunteers, assess community needs, and collaborate with other agencies?
- Do your executive leaders have regular conversations with staff, funding partners, investors, and beneficiaries to determine how you're doing at delivering on your brand promise.
- Do your executive leaders and Board meet with an exter-

nal facilitator on a regular basis (at least quarterly) for the purpose of strategic thinking and execution planning?

- How have demographic shifts impacted your nonprofit?
- What demographic shifts do you need to pay attention to?
- What impact will those shifts have on your organization?
- What are you doing now to proactively prepare for those shifts?
- How has your organization embraced and utilized technology and the web in how you raise funds, connect with volunteers, existing and potential investors, and tell your story?
- What impact would it have on your organization if you adopted an "Investor" mindset? How would that change things? Specifically what would have to change?

If you can't answer each of those questions with a comprehensive and clear response you've got some important work to do. Even if you have a clear and comprehensive response to some of those questions, you're not out of the woods. Strategic thinking and execution planning is an organizational way of life, not an isolated event or series of events.

As a certified Gravitas Coach, I've facilitated the very process I've outlined in this book with numerous nonprofit organizations and executive management teams. I know it works! I've seen it first hand time and time again as I've worked with both nonprofit and business clients. I happen to believe that our tools and process are second to none! They've proven to be effective with thousands of mid-growth companies spanning the globe! I first encountered Verne Harnish's book, Mastering the Rockefeller Habits as I was considering transitioning out of nonprofit executive leadership into forming my own consulting company. As I read Verne's book, I realized that the principles encompassed in the Four Decision-s™ Planning Model could work for nonprofit organizations. The model would need to be contextualized but the principles were sound. As I joined Gravitas Impact Premium Coaches and went through the certification process, I became even more convinced and evangelistic in my zeal to promote this planning model and invest myself in working with organizations like yours.

I doubt there's much that you've encountered in your read of this book that is completely new to you. It may be packaged differently but it's not unique to me by any stretch of the imagination. You are now accountable for what you know. You can do something with the information you now possess.

You were introduced to the Power of One Cash Management tool. There's another Power of One principle I'd like to remind you of and challenge you with. Any system, whether it's a family system, business system, or nonprofit system, has the potential to move towards positive growth and movement if one person within that system is prepared to take a step back from that system, gain a fresh perspective related to that system, and then re-engage that system, changing the way in which they relate to that system given that fresh perspective. You have at your disposal, the Power of One. You can be the one who is the catalyst for change in your organization. It's true! It really is! It will take courage on your part, persistence in engaging others within the system, motivated by a desire to see your organization not only survive but thrive! From personal experience, I know this to be true! I've seen as it I've led organizations similar to yours, and I've seen it as I've facilitated this process for other nonprofits.

You have a choice. Actually several choices. You can do nothing. If that's your choice, I would be sad, because I have much higher hopes for you. You can choose to be entrepreneurial by reaching out to someone who has the expertise, tools, and skill set to lead your organization through a strategic thinking/execution planning process. This choice will set you apart from many similar nonprofit organizations who are unwilling to think and act entrepreneurially. I believe that your long term survival is dependant on thinking and acting entrepreneurially. I'd be honored to hear more of your story and provide you with some personalized input. Visit my website at www.powerofoneconsulting.ca or the Gravitas ImpactPremiumCoacheswebsiteatwww.gravitasimpact.com access a coach in your geographic region. If their coaching focus does not include nonprofit organizations I know they'll put you in touch with a Gravitas Impact Premium Coach who can help

you transform your community .

SUGGESTED RESOURCES

Chaim   Governance as Leadership. Reframing the
                   Work of Nonprofit Boards
Collins, Jim   Good to Great
Collins, Jim   Good to Great for the Social Sector
Collins, Jim   Great by Choice
Collins, Jim   Building Company Vision
Goldsmith, Marshall What Got You Here Won't Get You There
Gugelev, Alice,   What's Your End Game
Stern, Andres
Harnish, Verne   Mastering the Rockefeller Habits
Harnish, Verne   Scaling Up
Heffernan, Margaret Willful Blindness
Mackey, John   Conscious Capitalism
Morino, Mario   Leap of Reason
Pallotta, Dan   Uncharitable
Smart, Geoff   Who
Wiseman, Lis   Multipliers
Grenny, Joseph,   Influencer: The New Science of Leading
Patterson, Kerry   Change
Maxfield, David
McMillan, Ron

ABOUT THE AUTHOR

Ken Thiessen founded Power of One Consulting in 2010 following 25 years working for and with nonprofits as a staff person and a Board member. He spent five years in an nonprofit executive leadership role resourcing 45 affiliated nonprofit organizations and agencies. He is a visionary leader who is a catalyst for change. He has an earned doctorate with a specialization in understanding organizations as systems. His doctoral project focused on understanding the role and function of power in faith based nonprofits. Coincidental with founding Power of One he joined Gravitas Impact Premium coache and received his Certified Coach designation in October 2010. Ken invests his time and energy coaching executive management teams and boards of growth-oriented, entrepreneurial nonprofit organizations, and businesses in strategic thinking/execution planning, organizational health and development, and team building.

Contact Information
Web - www.powerofoneconsulting.ca
Email - ken@powerofoneconsulting.ca
Twitter - @kenthiessen
LinkedIn - Ken Thiessen

POWER OF ONE CONSULTING
Transforming Communities One Nonprofit at a Time.

Kenaston House is not that much different than most nonprofit organizations. It's driven by a passionate commitment to a 'change the world' cause. Their executive leadership team and Board of Directors are convinced they're running an efficient operation and maximizing their desired impact to do good in the world. They're good, well-meaning people who share a deep passion for the cause they're invested in. If you're a nonprofit leader or Board member, that probably describes you and your organization.

What the Kenaston leadership team doesn't realize is there's a tsunami of epic proportions about to hit land that will threaten the organization's very existence. Prior to the tsunami's arrival, a smaller storm strikes the organization. The Executive Director, hired five years earlier to replace the retiring founder, takes a medical leave due to the stress of leading this dynamic organization in addressing real and significant community needs. That event reveals critical gaps which, if left unaddressed, threaten to end Kenaston's work in the city. A newly elected Board Chair, with a solid understanding of the Board's governance responsibility and an entrepreneurial way of exercising his duties, would prove pivotal for Kenaston's survival. The Board contracts an external consultant with a proven track record of working with nonprofit organizations, aware of their unique opportunities and challenges. The consultant employs a planning model designed to help Kenaston address the gaps. The strategic thinking process serves as the catalyst to help Kenaston maximize sustainable impact enabling the organization to scale up and thrive!

Weaving fable and theory, Dr. Ken Thiessen speaks to the heart of the issue facing most nonprofits today. Given the way in which the world is changing, the old way no longer works!

Many nonprofit leaders lie awake at night wrestling with that realization but are too afraid to think entrepreneurially. Ultimately that's the only way to avoid the tsunami about to hit your organization. It's also the key to maximizing sustainable impact for the people you care most about!
$25.95

www.ingramcontent.com/pod-product-compliance
Lightning Source LLC
Chambersburg PA
CBHW031811190326
41518CB00006B/283